Grassroots Governance in Germany and India

About the Authors

Prof. G. Palanithurai, Rajiv Gandhi Chair for Panchayati Raj Studies, and Dean, Students Welfare, Gandhigram Rural Institute, Gandhigram is an academic activist. He is specializing in grassroots governance and development. He closely works with local, regional and federal governments. He actively collaborates with civil society activities to strengthen Panchayati Raj System in India. He has developed a leadership school in Rajiv Gandhi Chair. To his credit he has sixty-five books, eighty-three monographs, seventy-six popular articles, one hundred and thirty-nine research articles in his area of specialization. He is a visiting Professor in Cologne University, Germany. He extensively travelled abroad in academic assignments. His action research activities were supported by the Ford Foundation, the Population Foundation of India, DANIDA, Rajiv Gandhi Foundation, UNDP, The Hunger Project, UNICEF, The World Bank, State Planning Commission, Action Aid International, Swiss Development and Cooperation, Toolkit Foundation Netherland and a few other agencies. He is the coordinator of the UGC Sponsored Innovative Programme and UGC Special Assistance Programme of the Department of Political Science and Development Administration, Gandhigram Rural Institute.

Mr. Niclas D. Weimar is teaching assistant in the Department of Indology, Cologne University, Germany. He is consultant to many organizations of Solar Energy. He has to his credit four research articles and three books. He is pursuing research in Cologne University, Germany.

Dr. Sonkhogin Haokip is Assistant Professor in the Department of Political Science and Development Administration, Gandhigram Rural Institute. He is specializing in decentralization process in the North East India. He has to his credit three books and seven research articles. He is currently doing an ICSSR Project.

GRASSROOTS GOVERNANCE IN GERMANY AND INDIA
A Comparative Analysis

G. PALANITHURAI
NICLAS D. WEIMAR
SONKHOGIN HAOKIP

CONCEPT PUBLISHING COMPANY PVT. LTD.
NEW DELHI-110059

ISBN-13 : 978-93-5125-013-5

First Published 2014

Published and Printed by

Concept Publishing Company Pvt. Ltd.
A/15-16, Commercial Block, Mohan Garden
New Delhi-110059 (India)
T: 25351460, 25351794, *F*: 091-11-25357109
E: publishing@conceptpub.com, W: www.conceptpub.com
Editorial Office: H-13, Bali Nagar, New Delhi-110 015, India.

Cataloging in Publication Data--*Courtesy:* D.K. Agencies (P) Ltd. <docinfo@dkagencies.com>

Palanithurai, G. (Ganapathy)
Grassroots governance in Germany and India : a comparative analysis / G. Palanithurai, Niclas D. Weimar, Sonkhogin Haokip.
p. cm.
Includes bibliographical references and index.
ISBN 9789351250135

1. Holzheim (Rhein-Lahn-Kreis, Germany)—Politics and government. 2. Local government—Germany—Rhineland-Palatinate. 3. Tellou Channa Seijang (India) Politics and government. 4. Panchayat—India—Manipur. I. Weimar, Niclas D., joint author. II. Haokip, Sonkhogin, 1978-, joint author. III. Title.

DDC 320.80943 23

Preface

Local Governance in Europe is different from Local Governance in India. Local government has many partners in Europe. Many of the services are provided by many players and not necessarily by the local body institutions alone and whereas in India local bodies in India have to discharge certain responsibilities and they are to be done only by the local bodies. In western setting local government means municipalities. They are almost urban in nature. They are local self government as their area of operation is well demarcated and enjoy greater autonomy. No confusion among the stakeholders about the roles to be performed by the federal government, provincial government and local government. Moreover, local government's resource mobilization capacity is strong in the West contrary to India. In India local governance is considered as spending institution. It will not take responsibility to mobilize resources internally. Further it has no capacity to do that exercise effectively.

Local governance institutions in the west are having the required capacity to perform their duties and responsibilities effectively and professionally. Service deliveries are being done by different agencies and they are being monitored by the local body institutions. These are the obvious points I have noticed when I was in Germany for six months as visiting faculty in Cologne University. Since I taught this subject in that university I have decided to compare the local governance operation in Germany with India by studying one local unit especially lowest unit in local governance in both countries.

Thus Holzheim, a small village in Rhiseland-Palatinate province has been selected from Germany and in the same way Tellou Channa Seijang Gram Panchayat from Manipur has been selected for this comparative analysis. Data have been collected from the field and they are analyzed and presented cogently and coherently to understand how strong the local governance institutions in Germany and India in terms of its structure, function and resources. The two institutions are functioning in two different institutional settings. They are to be given in a simple understandable framework to the students of masters who are undergoing programmes in local governance and with the above purpose this monograph is written.

Acknowledgements

Normally when I get an idea, it is my trait that I will immediately get into action. At one level it is easy if it is confined to the capacity of mine. But it is always beyond my capacity. I can generate idea, but to operationalise the same it requires a team work. I always believe in team work. When I was in Germany I have decided to compare one German village with one Indian village in terms of governance. So two case studies have to be conducted. Conducting a study in Germany that too in the rural areas I require the support of a German researcher. Luckily I found Mr. Niclas Weimar a teaching assistant in the Centre for Modern Indian Studies Cologne University who was assisting me when I was in Cologne University in Indology department.

Since he is an active researcher when I opened up this idea, he immediately responded positively that he would help me in collecting data from the Germany side. But I need such a study from Indian side and for which I was searching for a scholar to undertake the same. I found my collegue Mr. Sonkhogin Haokip working with me as Assistant Professor in the Department of Political Science and Development Administration, Gandhigram Rural Institute-Deemed University, Gandhigram. He did Ph.D. programme under my supervision. He also evinced keen interest but he told me that he would bring Manipur Experience in local governance. I have accepted and he also participated in this venture.

Hence, first I must thank both scholars who worked with me to bring out this monograph. Secondly, two units deserve my mention here. One is my colleagues and the other is my family. Both units are always with me in allowing me to carry out all types of academic, research and outreach activities. Thirdly, the Concept Publishing Company which deserves my appreciation as it is one of the companies which have published more number of titles on local governance in India. One can get more number of books on local governance from this company. Much of the works are drawn from the field. In such a way it has emerged as a specialist in publication. Hence, I must thank profusely Mr. Ashok Kumar Mittal and his sons for their committed action in this regard.

Gandhigram **G. Palanithurai**
07.06.2012

Contents

List of Tables, Diagrams and Maps

TABLES

DIAGRAMS

MAPS

Abbreviations

AoM	Association of Municipalities
CDU	Christian Democratic Union
EU	European Union
FRG	Federal Republic of Germany
FWG	Freie Wählergruppe
GDR	German Democratic Republic
MC	Municipal Council
MSI	Medium-Scale Industry
SME	Small and Medium Enterprise
SSI	Small-Scale Industry
SU	Soviet Union
USA	United States of America
USSR	Union of Soviet Socialist Republics
UN	United Nations
UNESCO	United Nations Educational, Scientific and Cultural Organization

Chapter I

Introduction

"Local governance" in the era of globalization of economy is a much debated and deliberated subject for the past three decades in the world. In the context of emerging movements of people in the world for democratization, local governance in more than eighty countries gained currency under the new initiative of "decentralization of power"[1]. Local governance is not a one prototype model for the whole world. There are many types and models. But a generic classification brings only two types of local governance in the world. Local governance in industrialized countries varies from local governance in developing countries[2]. Local governance in the developing countries is in the onward march of democratization of societies and communities and that too in a movement mode with a strong push from the state[3]. It is an initiative of the state and not the demand of the people. Perception varies from individual to individual about the new dispensation. Local governance of today is totally new with revolutionary characteristics compared to the old one.

But the local governance in the west is not new. It is old and stabilized. Before proceeding further it is necessary to differentiate local government from local governance. Local Government is an institution looking after some assigned

Table 1.1: Differences between Old Local Government and New Local Government

Sl. No.	Old Local Government	New Local Government
1.	It is the instrument of the state	It is based on subsidiarity
2.	It is based on *ultra vires*	It is based on community governance
3.	It is focused on government	It is focused on citizen
4.	It is an agent of the government	It is an agent of the citizens
5.	It is responsible and accountable to higher level government	It is responsible and accountable to citizens
6.	It is based on secrecy	It is based on transparency
7.	It is output oriented	It is outcome oriented
8.	It is rules driven	It is result driven
9.	It is target oriented	It is process oriented
10.	It is mechanical	It is organical
11.	It is exclusive with elite capture	It is inclusive participatory

responsibilities. Local governance is a process of performing certain services with the participation of many agencies to the community including local government. Now we use the term local governance as it is popular now as local delivery services are done by many agencies with the overall supervision of local governments.

The new dispensation in India has got certain new tasks and responsibilities[4]. Primarily democratization of the society, achieving social justice, economic development of the poor, establishing participatory planning and governance, empowering the marginalized is the major goals with which new local governance system has been established. It is to be recognized that the new local governance arrangement has been established through amending the Constitution of India and by which it becomes a permanent entity in the governance orbit of the Indian political system. It is necessary that enabling conditions have to be created by different stakeholders to get the full benefit from the local governance as the system has got tremendous potentials. In the Afro-Asian settings and more particularly in India new local governance has to face volley of challenges as it is not only an institutional mechanism to deliver services but essentially and primarily it has to work for social justice and empowerment by transferring power from the dominant to oppressed class[5]. Here it is necessary to trace the base argument for the establishment of new Panchayati Raj or rural local governance in India. At the dawn of independence the discussion was initiated on Panchayati Raj by M.K. Gandhi in the context of establishing governance system for India[6]. As he visualized a new pattern of governance for this country he developed a base argument that governance system for India should start from grassroots. He had come to this conclusion based on the evaluation of the governance system in the world. He evaluated more specifically the western governance pattern and brought to light the characteristics of the system. Since our founding fathers were inclined to adopt the western model of government[7], he indicated the weaknesses of the above system. The characteristics of modern democracy are given in Diagram 1.1.

After seeing the drawback he has established his framework of governance which is called Gram Swaraj or Village Swaraj. The characteristics of the above framework are given in Diagram 1.2.

In Village Swaraj how citizen has to perform has been codified and explained. For the Village Swaraj maturity of the citizens are essential. To bring such condition a group of intelligent people should work continuously by creating awareness and sensitising them (Diagram 1.3).

While doing so he underlined how citzens should be in the society. Now the people are under the control of the government through its departments. Nearly thirty-seven government departments are working in the rural areas. They

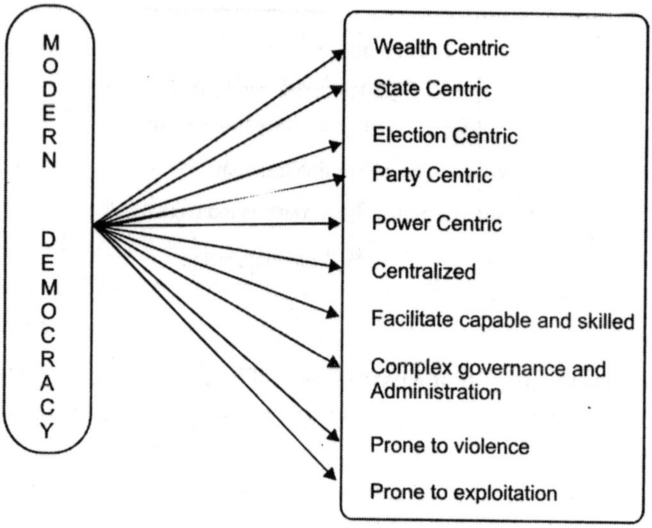

Diagram 1.1: Modern Democracy

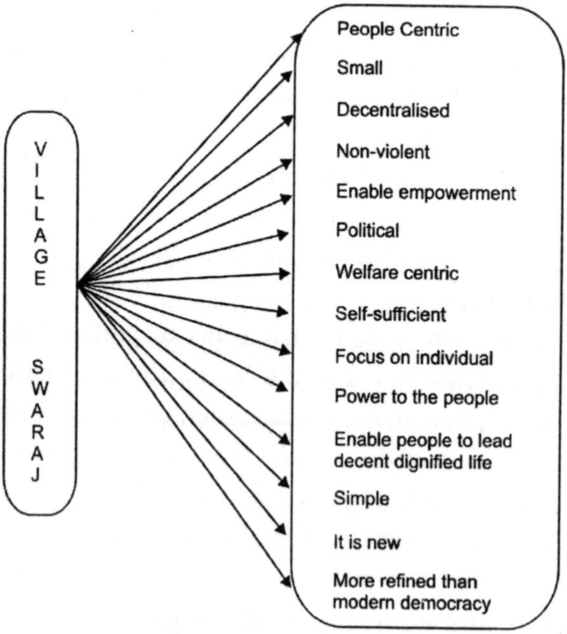

Diagram 1.2: Village Swaraj

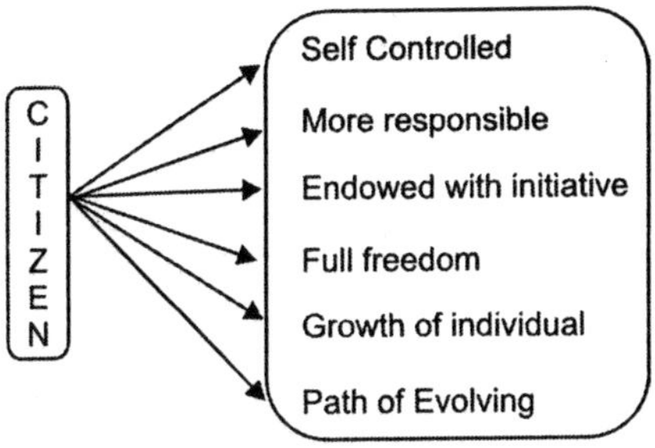

Diagram 1.3: Citizen

have roles and responsibilities. They carry out series of development programmes for the benefit of the people. Despite their best efforts by investing huge resource they could not achieve what the government wanted to achieve. But successfully people are brought under the control of the government officials. Many of the occasions government departments are sitting on the shoulders of the people. That is why people and more particularly the poor are bringing an argument that they are supported or oppressed. (Diagram 1.4)

In a true democracy government should be under the control of the people. Since people have been oriented to behave as beneficiaries, they are continuously made as powerless. When people are unable to get the assured benefits, they will be made to become the petitioners. Further they are made powerless. In order to change the paradigm he developed a new framework. In the new framework he made the whole governance exercise from the perspective of people. It is totally people centric. (Diagram 1.5)

In this framework M.K. Gandhi identified the essential aspects of an ideal village. They are given below in the form of Diagram 1.6.

M.K. Gandhi's framework of governance was not acceptable to our political pandits at the dawn of independence

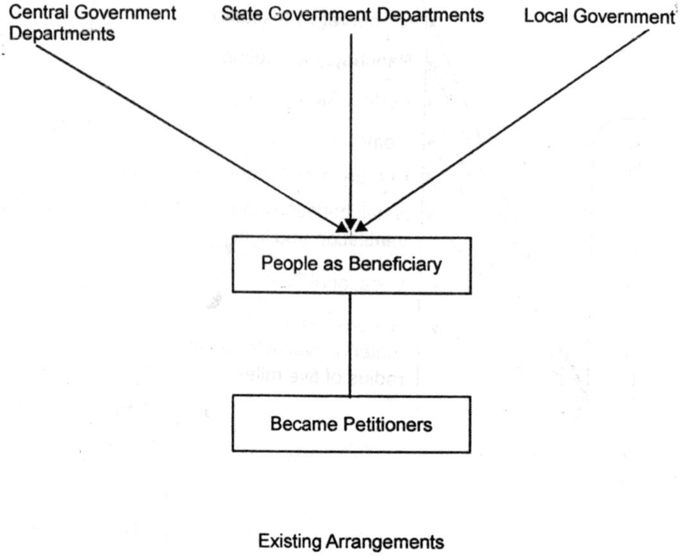

Diagram 1.4: Structure of Governments

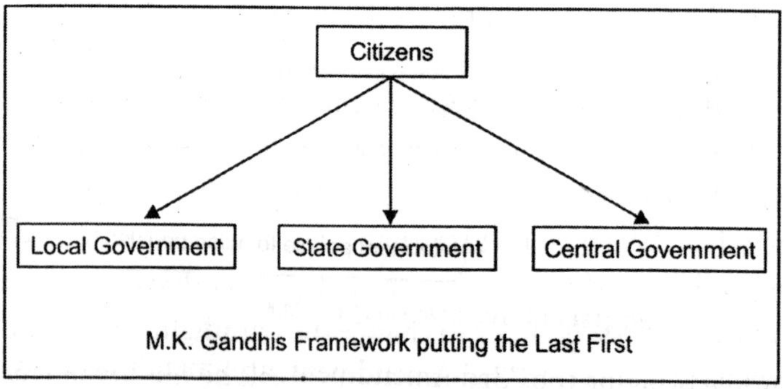

Diagram 1.5: M.K. Gandhi's Framework

as many believed that the state would transform the society. But after the forty years of experience in democratic governance many realized that the state has failed miserably. In this context the modern managers of new India were in search of alternatives. While they were searching for alternative, they found the Gandhian framework of local governance.

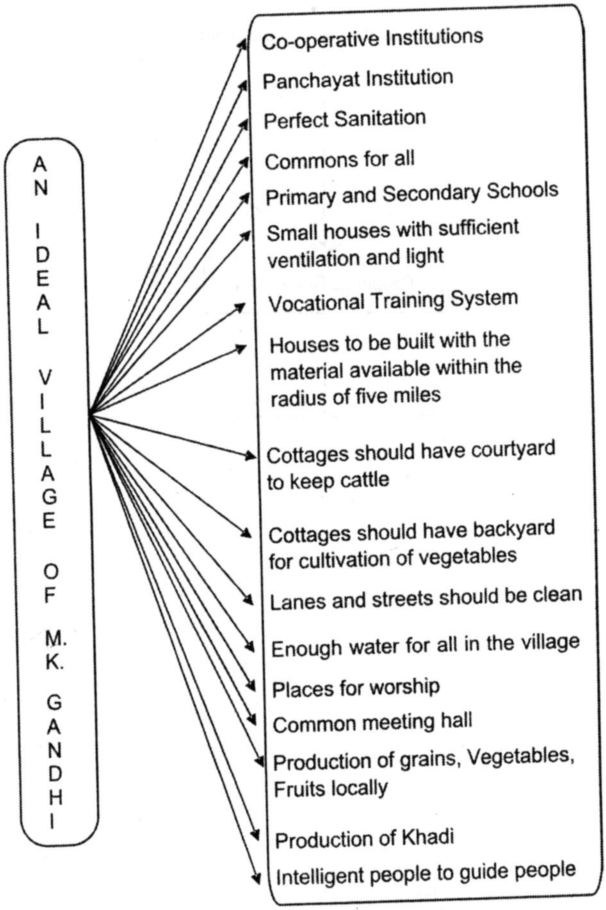

Diagram 1.6: An Ideal Village of M.K.Gandhi

While bringing the 73rd Amendment, arguments have been projected as M.K. Gandhi brought arguments for the establishment of village Swaraj. Rajiv Gandhi in all his speeches brought the arguments of M.K. Gandhi for Panchayati Raj[8]. If anyone looks carefully the 73rd Amendment to the Constitution of India, most of the key characteristics of the Gandhian framework are in the 73rd Amendment. To look at decentralisation we need perspective. The characteristics are given in Diagram 1.7:

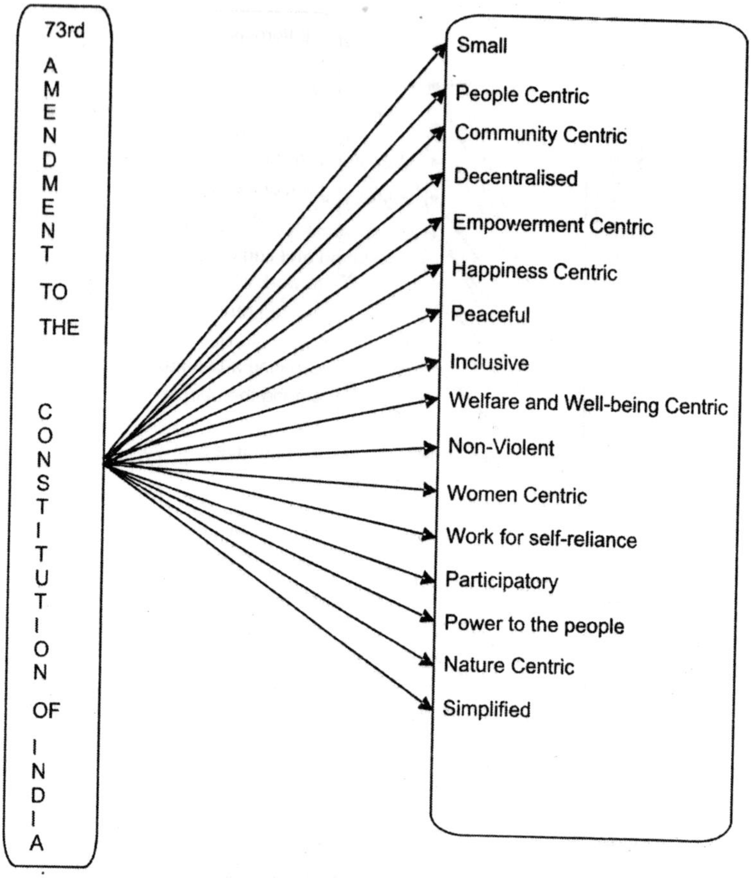

Diagram 1.7: 73rd Constitutional Amendment of India

To operationalise the 73rd Amendment in letter and spirit an array of steps are essential[9]. They are given in Diagram 1.8.

But to operationalise the whole scheme of rural local governance at present transformative leadership is crucial. The characteristics of a transformative leader are given in Diagram 1.9.

The effective functioning of local governance that too in rural India depends on a number of factors and of which

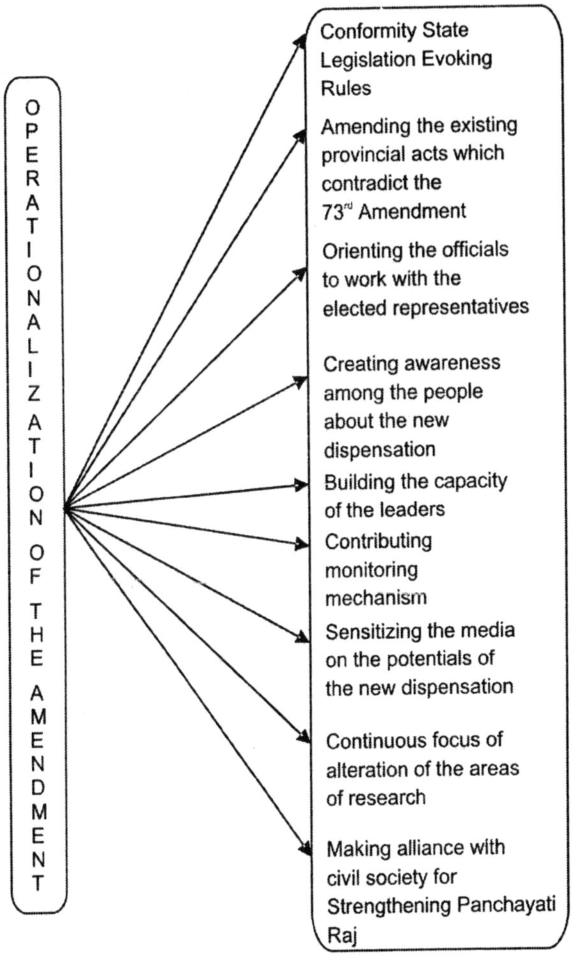

Diagram 1.8: Operationalisation of the Amendment

capacity of the local institutions and their representatives are primary. While making an analysis and evaluation of the local body institutions in India for the past one and half decades one can find hope and despair[10]. Basically wherever the elected representatives are skilled and capable, a transformative process is fast and effective and delivery of services are also effective. Hence, leadership plays an important role in

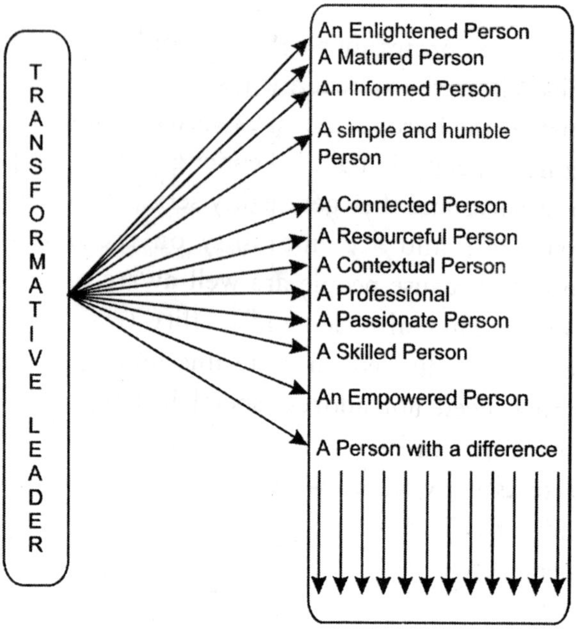

Diagram 1.9: Transformative Leader

translating the objective of new rural local governance into the reality[11]. The leadership should be transformatory and they should have vision, commitment, sincerity and skill and more particularly commitment in honesty and democracy. It cannot be presumed that all elected representatives will have all the above mentioned characteristics. In order to bring such characteristics the elected representatives should be oriented, trained, and sensitized on the values of democracy. Social justice and equitable development. Further resource base of the local bodies is yet another factor for strengthening local bodies and effective functioning of the same[12]. Steps should to be taken continuously to reform local governance for effective functioning[13].

In Europe the task is different and to perform the task the

system requires professionals. Since people are with needed awareness about the system, the task of the system becomes easy. Further the Europe's Local Governance system resource mobilizing capacity is high[14]. People generally prepared to pay for services and they get quality service. One could find responsiveness and accountability on the part of local government. Because people are well aware of the systems functioning. They also demand quality service. People in Europe are not divided on caste line and hence the local governance need not address social justice issue. Gender disparity is not an issue and hence there is no necessity to reserve seats for women. Women are contesting along with men and got elected to the bodies. Look at local governance using perspectives are more important.

There are five perspectives to look at local governance models. They are: (a) Fiscal Federalism, (b) New Public Management (NPM), (c) Public Choice, (d) New Institutional Economics, and (e) Network Forms of Local Governance. All these perspectives deal with market failures, state failures and new institutional arrangements to overcome both failures. The new framework envisages responsive, responsible and accountable governance through the initiatives of the representatives of the people and by the participation of the people. In the whole world one could find verieties of local government's. As per the characteristics, they are classified as models.

There are different models of local governance in the world. They are: the Nordic model, the Swiss model, the French model, the German model, the British model, the Indian model, the Chinese model, the Japanese model, the North American model and the Australian model.

This study compares the German model with the Indian

model. Hence, a brief description is given below for common understanding of both models. German model emphasizes the principle of subsidiary, cooperation and administrative efficiency. It provides responsibilities of service delivery to the local governments. But a great deal of autonomy is given to local government in the area of service delivery. Local government expenditure constitutes about 10 per cent of GDP. Indian Local Government model has a strong historical tradition. It has several functions from management of land, commons, temples, taxation, and dispute resolution and so on. But it was weakened over a period of time. After independence also the Panchayati Raj System has not been strengthened. It has been made as an instrument of the State government to carry out the programmes and schemes of the Central and State governments. Local government expenditures constitute not even 1 per cent of GDP.

Here in this study, for a common understanding of the students German model has been studied and explained broadly through a case study conducted at the lowest unit of local body arrangement. In the same way local governance system more specifically rural local body system has been studied and explained through a case analysis of a village Panchayat in India. For this study a simple framework has been adopted. Institutional structures, powers assigned, roles and responsibilities given to the institutional structures, resources devolved and performance exhibited through the institutions by the institutional leaders are analysed in both case studies.

REFERENCES

1. Satyajit Singh and Pradeep K. Sharma (eds.), *Decentralization: Institutions and Politics in Rural India,* New Delhi: Oxford

University Press, 2007; Niraja Gopal Jayal, Amit Prakash and Pradeep K. Sharma (eds.), *Local Governance in India: Decentralization and Beyond,* New Delhi: Oxford University Press, 2006; and Pranab Bardhan and Dilip Mookherjee (eds.), *Decentralization and Local Governance in Developing Countries : A Comparative Perspective,* New Delhi: Oxford University Press, 2007.

2. Anwar Shah (ed.), *Local Governance in Industrial Countries,* Washington DC: The World Bank, 2006; Anwar Shah (ed.), *Local Governance in Developing Countries,* Washington DC: The World Bank, 2006.
3. James Manor, *The Political Economy of Democratic Decentralization,* Washington DC: The World Bank, 1999.
4. Institute of Social Sciences, *Status of Panchayati Raj in the States and Union Territories of India 2000,* New Delhi: Concept Publishing Company, 1994.
5. Rakesh Hooja and Sunil Dutt (eds.), *Fifty Years of Panchayati Raj and Decentralised Development,* New Delhi: Indian Institute of Public Administration, 2010.
6. M.K.Gandhi, *Village Swaraj,* Ahmedabad; Navajivan Publishing House, 1962.
7. AVARD, *Panchayat Raj as the Basis of Indian Polity: An Exploration into the Proceedings of the Constituent Assembly*, New Delhi, Association of Voluntary Agencies for Rural Development,1962.
8. G. Palanithurai, *Rajiv Gandhi's Vision on Local Governance,* New Delhi: Concept Publishing Company Pvt. Ltd. New Delhi, 2009.
9. G. Palanithurai, *Decentralisation in India: Critical Issues from the Field,* New Delhi: Concept Publishing Company Pvt. Ltd. New Delhi, 2009.
10. Institute of Rural Management Anand, *State of Panchayat Report 2008-2009: An Independent Assessment*, New Delhi: Ministry of Panchayati Raj, Government of India, 2010 Vols I & II; Second Administrative Reforms Commission, *Local*

Governance: An Inspiring Journey into the Future (6th Report), New Delhi: Government of India, 2007.

11. G. Palanithurai, M.A.Thirunavukkarasu and G. Uma, *Change Makers at Grassroots: Leadership Matters Much,* New Delhi: Concept Publishing Company Pvt. Ltd. New Delhi, 2010; Jayshree Mangubhai, Aloysius Irudayam. Sj and Emma Sydenham, *Dalit Women's Right Political Participation in Rural Panchayati Raj*, Netherland: Dalit Research Programme, 2009.
12. Anwar Shah (ed.), *Local Budgeting*, Washington DC: The World Bank, 2007.
13. The World Bank, *Fiscal Decentralization to Rural Government in India*, New Delhi: Oxford University Press, 2004.
14. Commission on Centre – State Relations, *Report on Local Self Government and Decentralized Governance*, New Delhi: Government of India, 2010; Second Administrative Reforms Commission, *Citizen Centric Administration: The Heart of Governance,* Vol. 12, New Delhi: Government of India, 2009.

Chapter II

Local Governance in Germany

PART I

Background: Federal Republic of Germany

The Federal Republic of Germany is a country in Central Europe. It has a territorial size of over 350,000 square kilometres, being one of the largest European countries after France, Spain and Sweden (not including Russia and Ukraine). By 2011, Germany's population exceeded 81 million people and is thus the most populous country in the European Union. About 25 per cent of Germany's population live in rural areas. Nearly 10 per cent of her population is foreigners and about 20 per cent have immigrant roots. Thanks to her strong economy, Germany has been a popular destination for emigrational influx. Germany borders clockwise Denmark, Poland, the Czech Republic, Austria, Switzerland, France, Luxembourg, Belgium and the Netherlands.

Over two-thirds of the German population are Christians and about 50 per cent of them Catholic and the other nearly 50 per cent Protestants. The second largest religion is Islam, which has been the result of large immigration from the Middle East to Germany in the past decades. The official language of the Federal

Map 2.1: Germany and its 16 States

Source: http://www.mapzones.org/maps/germany/Hamburg_Germany.gif (Adaption)

Republic of Germany is German with totally over 100 million speakers worldwide. It is also the official language in Austria and Liechtenstein and co-official language in Switzerland, Luxembourg, Belgium and South Tirol in Italy. German is one of the 23 official languages of the EU. There is also a considerable minority of Frisian and some Danish and Sorbian speakers as well as immigrant languages like Russian and Turkish.

Brief History of Germany

Parts of today's Germany on the Western shore of the river

Rhine were historically part of Roman Empire which heavily struggled with the Germanic tribes at the east of this natural border. Particularly famous is the defeat of several Roman legions to Arminius, the leader of a Germanic tribe in the year 9 C.E. In the course of the loss of power of the Roman Empire from the second century, these tribes step by step invaded and occupied Roman territory and even reached Rome. In 800, Charles the Great (Charlemagne) founded the Carolingian Empire which soon after his death split up, resulting in the creation of the Holy Roman Empire covering Central and South Europe and France covering Western Europe. After centuries of feudalism and prospering towns particularly in the Northern part as well as an increase in power of principalities and dukedoms, the black death, which originated from China and made its way to Europe after the breakup of the Islamic European-Asian trade blockage by the Mongolians, eradicated a large percentage of the population in the empire.

A major historical event was Martin Luther's challenge of the Roman Catholic Church with his 95 Theses he published in Wittenberg in 1517, which after Gutenberg's introduction of the printing press to Central Europe became easily and quickly widespread, thus triggering the Protestant Reformation that later culminated in the devastating Thirty Years' War (1618–1648). The end of the war led to a split up of the empire between the fractions of many independent principalities. The empire was finally dissolved in the course of the rise of Napoleon of France and the Napoleonic Wars. After Napoleon's fall, the German Confederation was founded as a loose association of several principalities. This loose structure was not stable enough to sustain against disputes and conflicts, thus after several decades of conflicts and struggles, most importantly the 1864 war of Austria and Prussia against Denmark and the 1866 war of brothers between Austria and Prussia, Prussia eventually gained the upper hand not only internally but also externally against the common arch enemy France, which after her defeat in the Franco-Prussian war had to accept the proclamation of the German Empire in 1871 in Versailles. In the course of colonial activism of other European powers like Great Britain and France, Germany long time abstained from getting colonies and only engaged in the late nineteenth century for not more than three decades into the colonialization of parts of Central and Southwest Africa, China as well as of Samoa and New Guinea in the Pacific.

When the crown prince of Austria was assassinated in 1914, Germany supported Austria in her war against Serbia, triggering World War I. The four years' war ended with the defeat of Germany and Austria as well as the Ottoman Empire and their respective humiliation by the Allies in the so called Diktatfrieden (dictated peace), which later greatly helped Hitler make his way to power. The defeat culminated into the German revolution in 1918 and the abdication of the last emperor William II, thus leading to the establishment of the Weimar Republic. The hard conditions of the Versailles Treaty as well as the global economic depression, which led to large unemployment in Germany, brought about an increase in popularity of the National Socialist Party and their leader Adolf Hitler. The party and its leader managed to grasp power in Germany and centralize the state. The German government started to re-acquire formerly lost German territories and build up her military capacities. After having annexed Austria and Czechoslovakia, the invasion of Poland on 1st September, 1939 became the starting point of the devastating World War II, during which not only millions of soldiers and civilians were killed, but also millions of Jews fell victim to the fascist ideology of the Nazis. After Hitler's death, the war ended in 1945 with the occupation of Germany by the United Kingdom, France, the USA and the USSR.

The mounting dispute between the western allies and the USSR led to a split of Germany into East and West Germany, which both after only few years of administration by their respective occupational powers became two independent states. While West Germany established a federal parliamentary republic, the German Democratic Republic (GDR) – East Germany – became a Soviet style one-party state. The fierce ideological conflict between the two blocs particularly centred on their European border in Berlin, resulting in the build up (construction) of the Berlin Wall in 1961. It was only in the 1970s that tensions between the two German states could eventually be reduced and after the collapse of the Soviet Union, East Germany was also no longer economically viable, resulting in the unification of East and West Germany into the Federal Republic of Germany in 1990. The capital city then also moved from Bonn to Berlin.

Rhineland-Palatinate Province

Rhineland-Palatinate lies in West Germany, bordering Belgium, France and Luxembourg. The state is an artificial construct established by the allied powers after World War II. It was part of the French Occupation Zone and made up of several former German district governments, regions and provinces. Its capital city is Mainz and as of 2011 had a population of nearly 4 million people. The federal state is home to a wide range of cultural and historical monuments and sites that are under protection by UNESCO. Economically, the state is famous for its wine growing culture that traces back to Roman time as well as its chemical and automobile industry. It is also a very popular destiny of tourism in Germany.

Local Governance Framework

After a brief historical introduction to local governance in Germany, this chapter will outline the current administrative hierarchy of the Federal Republic of Germany (FRG), the constitutional position of village governance and an analysis of the weakness and features of the current system.

Historical Background of Local Governance in Germany

Self-government is a characteristic form of local governance in German villages that has long historical roots. In the early Middle Ages, communes were more and more given self-government rights by the rulers or their respective small kingdoms, principalities, dukedoms, etc. These given rights initiated a centuries-long process of increasing autonomy of the local governments in terms of market liberty, construction of houses and walls, self-jurisdiction and lastly coinage. Following this development, cities became increasingly richer and more powerful with traders and craftsmen occupying strong and influential positions. Their growing prestige and significance triggered their organization into guilds and brotherhoods, which collaborated with the local government administration of their respective cities.[1]

In 1835 in the Kingdom of Prussia, the "revised Prussian City Order" stipulated the outlines of self-governance in the German states. Another development was the increase in honorary participation by villagers and citizens in the local government process, leading to the integration of non-professionals in public administration, which applies to corporate bodies under state supervision. Coining the different forms of self-governance in Germany, the various types comprise: economic self-governance in the corporate bodies of the chambers of commerce, crafts or agriculture; self-governance of professions in forms of associational organization of people from their respective professions; cultural self-governance of universities and other academics; social self-governance in the form of social security institutions for health, accident, unemployment, pensions, etc.; local self-governance, which has become an integral and prominent part in the administrative hierarchy of the FRG after World War II.[2]

Village Administration in Germany

Administrative Division of Germany

The administrative division of Germany is due to the country's federal structure and the deep historical roots of this federalism complicated and cannot be comprehensively outlined in few sentences. Thus, a rather short and simple attempt of classifying the German administrative system is made by particularly putting emphasis on the federal state where the caste study village is located.

German is a federal country divided into 13 federal states as well as three city-states. Five of these federal states are subdivided into Government Districts (*Regierungsbezirke*), while other neither have government districts or abolished them, such as the Federal State of Rhineland-Palatinate. Below government district-level there are urban and rural districts (so-called *Stadtkreise* and *Landkreise*) as well as district-free cities (*distriktfreie Städte*). In those federal states without government districts, the urban and rural districts are at the next highest administrative level below the federal state level. In some federal states, such as Rhineland-Palatinate, there are associations of municipalities between the urban/rural districts and the local municipalities, the latter which are villages and at the lowest administrative level in Germany. Following figure basically shows the administrative pyramid of the Federal Republic of Germany with emphasis on the structure in Rhineland-Palatinate at the sub-federal states-level.

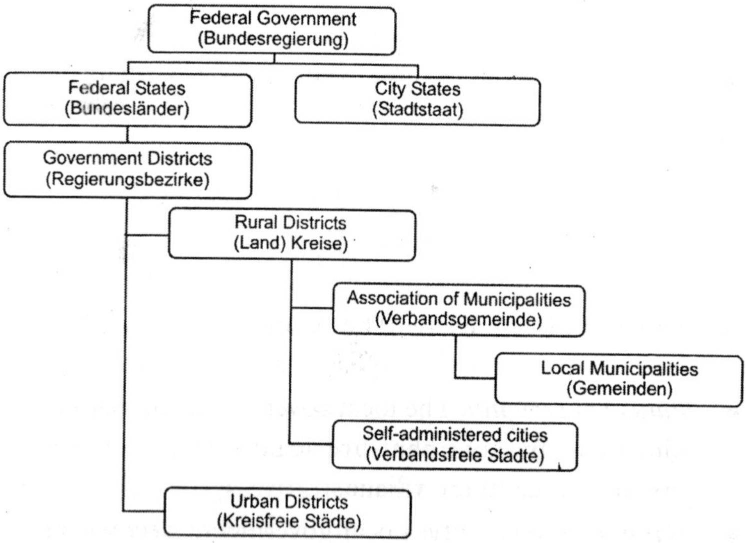

Diagram 2.1: Administrative division of Germany

Ortsgemeinden — Local Municipalities: Village Governance in Rhineland-Palatinate

The German Basic Law (*Grundgesetz*) stipulates a division of competences between the state government and the federal states. In this regard, local governance in Germany is regulated individually by the constitutions of the 16 federal states. Although the administrative arrangements and regulations for local governance differ from federal state to federal state, the Basic Law, however, requires all federal states to meet some basic principles, which are adherence to democratic principles, social governance based on the rule of law as well as free, equal and secret elections of the local representative organs — village council — by the locals.

Although there are different local government laws in each of the 16 federal states, there is a bunch of basic principles that are valid for all municipalities in the country in order to be enabled to carry out their work[3]:

- *Territorial Sovereignty*: The local government exercises sovereignty within its territory.
- *Personal Sovereignty*: The local government decides on its own on how many and who to employ.
- *Organisational Sovereignty*: The local government has the right to set up its own organisational structure.
- *Financial Sovereignty*: The local government can determine receipts and expenditures themselves.
- *Status Sovereignty*: The local government can release additional by-laws that are legally valid for the territorial area of the village.
- *Planning Sovereignty*: Local government decides on its own on the planning of construction projects or extension of residential areas.

In the case of the German federal state of Rhineland-Palatinate, local governance can truly be regarded as local as compared to other state. In the 1969 promulgated local government reforms, the state government in Mayence did not — like in other federal states — subsume the small municipalities into large municipalities, which would have erased village self-administration in the state, but introduced the administrative level of association of municipalities. According to § 68 Abs. 1 of the local municipality act (*Gemeindeordnung*), these associations primarily handle administrative and organizational work of a bunch of small municipalities, while the local municipalities themselves have their own councils and mayors, independently taking their own decisions on village development.[4] In that way, the small local municipalities could preserve their administrative independence while administrational work became at the same time more efficient.

The association of municipalities are responsible for affairs and matters that affect aspects such as school education, construction of sports and leisure time facilities as well as social protection and elderly care centres, technical support and fire protection, water supply and wastewater management. The AOM carry out a large bunch of secretarial and administrative work of the municipalities, covering matters such as issue of identity cards or resident's registration. They are also governed by an elected council, presided by a full-time mayor. The mayor of an AOM can be mayor of other local municipalities at the same time.

The councils of the local municipalities are constituted through elections, organized and carried out locally. An elected council decides about all matters and affairs that affect the village and pertaining areas, starting from construction projects, cooperation, festivals or waste management and have their own financial budget constituted by land, house and corporate taxes.

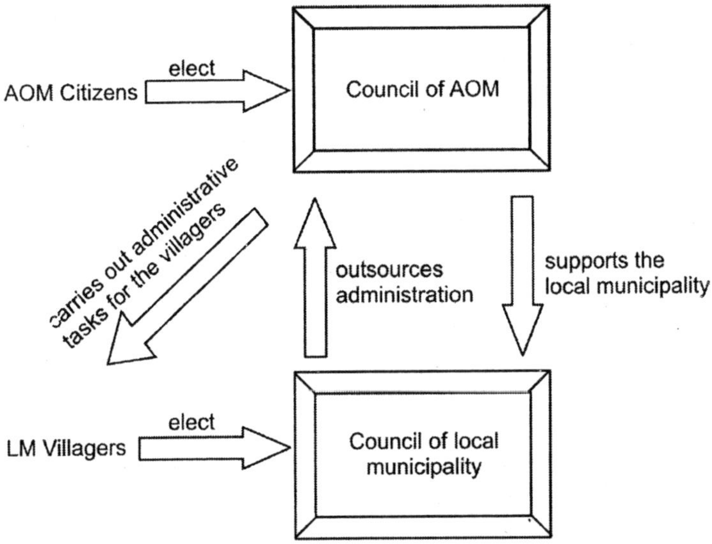

Diagram 2.2: Relationship between Local Municipality and Association of Municipalities

Currently, there is an administrative reform process of local governance taking place in Rhineland-Palatinate, which aims at the optimization of the administrative and territorial structures and an increase in efficiency of governance in the state. Accordingly, one step foresees that district-free local municipalities and association of municipalities will be integrated into others that pertain to a district.

PART II

Local Governance in Action

Introduction

As case study for local governance in Germany, the small village Holzheim in the state Rhineland-Palatinate was selected due to the special character of villages in this Western German states, which is — as compared to the majority of German villages in other states — their high degree of administrative autonomy. After a brief introduction to the historical background of the village, Holzheim's characteristics village will be outlined. Subsequently, the chapter proceeds to analyse the process and performance of local governance in that German village.

Panoramic view over Holzheim from the hillside

Historical Background of Holzheim

The history of Holzheim dates back over 1200 years. It was first mentioned in records on 24 September 772, when ten morgen[5] of land in Lahngau, Walesheim and Holzheim were bestowed to the Lorch Monastery[6]. Holzheim's history is narrowly characterized by its hill-built castle — now in ruins — called Ardeck, which is today a listed cultural monument under protection of the state government.[7] For the villagers of Holzheim, Ardeck is a symbol of home land. It was built by Earl Adolph of Diez and Nassau. The first available documents about Ardeck can be found in the chronicles of Tileman Ehlen von Wolfhagen, dated 1395. The chronicles also report about an earlier castle that had been built on the same site. Ardeck presumably functioned as a border fortification against the Shire of Katzenelnbogen, but later increasingly served as private residence for its owners. It was inhabited until 1727 when the family lineage died out and abandoned Ardeck, which over the centuries became decomposed.[8]

The Castle Ardeck

During and after the Thirty Years War (1618 – 1648), economic and social problems as well as increasing poverty and security problems motivated more and more people to emigrate from Central Europe to Eastern Europe, Czarist Russia, Argentina, Brazil, Australia and North America. The mass emigration wave did also not stop at Holzheim, from where — particularly since the Mid-nineteenth century — several villagers migrated to America. Researched records account for more than three dozen emigrated villagers.

Administratively, Holzheim was until the late fourteenth century part of the Shire of Diez, but then became part of Nassau Dillenburg when the earl died without male successors. After a short period of occupation by the French in 1795, Holzheim was integrated into the Dukedom of Nassau, which itself was after the German War of 1866 annexed by the Kingdom of Prussia. With the establishment of the German Reich in 1871, Holzheim became incorporated into the Province of Hesse — Nassau. During World War II. (1939 – 1945), Holzheim was one of the many showcases of military confrontation between the Allies and German Wehrmacht soldiers. Old villagers today still report about a fatal bombing of a train passing through the village in 1944 that allegedly carried weaponry. The bombing not only killed many combatants but also several Holzheim citizens who used to hide in bunkers or the cellars of their houses. After the Reich's dissolution following Germany's defeat in World War II., Holzheim became in 1946 a part of the newly created area of Rhineland-Palatinate of France's Military Occupation Zone in West Germany. In 1949, Rhineland-Palatinate joined as federal state the newly established Federal Republic of Germany.

After 1945, more than 100 war refugees found a new home in Holzheim, at that time about one-seventh of the village population. For them it was very difficult in the post-war times to integrate into the new environment and build up their existence in a largely destroyed country. However, the economic upturn in Germany since the 1950s, denominated as the economic miracle of Germany, helped to increase wealth among the population at a fast pace. The population in Holzheim also grew by 250 people. Yet, increasing economic development also changed the economic structures of Holzheim from a predominantly agrarian village to a rather residential village with only few farmers. The development and increasing population in the village likewise led to a modernization of streets, mechanization of the remaining agrarian sector and construction of new family houses and thus residential areas in the late 1960s. In 1986, the planning phase for a commercial area in the upper hill-side part of the village at the entrance from the direction of Limburg started. In the following decades, this resulted in the establishment of both small local companies as well as large international enterprises like DiaSys with headquarters in Holzheim and offices in world cities like Shanghai (China) and Kobe (Japan), also providing jobs for several residents from Holzheim and nearby villages. The idyllic location of the village in the green, its good connection to neighbouring cities, railway stations and even airports as well as the local commercial areas have made Holzheim a very attractive place to live, yet forcing the local administration to restrict the construction of new houses in order to curb any development of the village becoming too urbanized.

Winter Scenery in Holzheim

Basic Facts about the Village

Holzheim is a small village in the federal state of Rhineland-Palatinate, bordering the federal state of Hesse. Administratively, the village is defined as a *Ortsgemeinde* (municipality) that belongs to the *Verbandsgemeinde* (association of municipalities – AOM) of Diez which itself is part of the Rhein-Lahn district (German: *Kreis*). The village lies in natural valley on the hillside, surrounded by farmland and a forest. Along the village flows the small river Aar that encompasses over a distance of 50 kilometres from the Taunus region in Hesse to Diez where it joins the river Lahn. Via road B54 across steep hills and farming land, Holzheim is at a flight distance of three kilometres connected to the city of Limburg in Hesse, which is a major traffic and employment hub for nearby villages and townships. Not only there are many small and medium enterprises (SMEs) and public offices in Limburg, but also highly advanced infrastructural linkages. Limburg has both a central railway station as well as a high speed train railway station to Cologne, Frankfurt and Heidelberg for instance. The city adjoins Germany's second largest highway A3 connecting the city with major German cities such as Frankfurt — only about 60 kilometres distance to Frankfurt International Airport, shortly: Fraport, the largest employer in Hesse – Koblenz, Rhineland-Palatinate's state capital Mainz or Hesse's state capital Wiesbaden. Likewise, B54 links Holzheim with other villages such as Flacht, Hahnstätten and Niederneisen and the township of Diez with its regionally famous castles and palaces, such as the Oranienstein Palace.

Holzheim covers an area of about seven square kilometres plus 176 hectares of forest. In addition to this, the castle ruin

Satellite view of Holzheim

of Ardeck belongs since 1986 to Holzheim. By December 2010, the village had a population of 864 people.[9] The overwhelming majority of the people of Holzheim — the Holzheimer — are ethnic Germans with only few foreigners from Austria and the former Soviet Union — so-called *Spätaussiedler* (German resettlers from the former Soviet Union) — living in the village. Later during 1990 the village experienced an influx of many non-locals and non-natives, who obtained land from some farmers and constructed new houses in the upper part of the village. These new residents have been particularly attracted by the formidable location of the village within green and natural scenery, yet offering very good infrastructure and connectivity to the neighbouring cities of Limburg and Diez. However, the current demographic trend shows that the population is decreasing with villagers moving out of the village every year due to their jobs or studies. Since most of the villagers prefer to drive by car, motorcycles are rarely seen in the village and predominantly only young people drive low-speed mopeds before meeting the age qualification for the car driving licence.

Forest of Holzheim with private fishing pond

Table 2.1: Basic Statistics about Holzheim

Total area	*7.0 sq. km*	*Population Details*	
Adjacent forest area	176 ha	Gender	Population
Population	864 people	Male	439
Density	123 people/ sq. km	Female	425
Literacy	100%	Total	864

Public Facilities and Village Economy

Holzheim comprises a wide range of public and gastronomical facilities that cover most of the everyday needs of the villagers. Apart from a bank, a library with a large inventory comprising more than 10,000 books and other media as well as a municipal hall which serves as the office of Holzheim's Mayor and meeting room for the local government body, the village also has a community hall where different cultural activities, weddings and musical and theatre events are conducted. Further public facilities include a large cemetery with a special corner for villagers that died during World War II. as well as water supply facility that is jointly operated with other neighbouring villages belonging to AOM of Diez. Previously, there was also an elementary school in Holzheim — closed in the 1970s — in what is now-a-days the municipal hall and library. There are two restaurants in the village of which one is regionally famous for its roasted chicken. The latter also functions as meeting point for various local clubs and associations. It has for decades provided a room with piano to Holzheim's choirs and musical associations. There is also a small pub where the aged male population meet up for a beer and watching football. It serves also as folklore meeting point during fun fair festivals. Holzheim even has a very small guest house. Until the late 1990s, Holzheim there were also a small shop as well as a bakery, yet these two facilities fell victim to the fierce competition against larger and low-cost offers from neighbouring cities. Since all households possess of cars, it is very easy and convenient for the villagers to drive to the nearby supermarkets, bakeries and butcheries to obtain fresh and also cheap food. For those villagers who are not capable of driving, particularly young people without driving licence and the older people, Holzheim is very well connected by regular buses with the neighbouring villages and townships and cities of Diez and Limburg.

Although there is neither a hospital nor a local health station in Holzheim, two physicians reside in the village and in urgent emergency cases provide medical assistance to sick villagers and in the neighbourhood. Both the physicians — a father and his son — provide a medical practice in the local municipality of Niederneisen, only three kilometres distance away from Holzheim. Yet, there is a very skilled veterinarian with a medical practice in the village, frequented by villagers and even citizens from Holzheim's surroundings.

Economy of Holzheim

Having been an agricultural village for centuries, Holzheim became in the course of the post-War twentieth century increasingly an industrialized village. The local economy these

The Community Hall of Holzheim

Table 2.2: Overview of Public and Gastronomical Facilities in Holzheim

Facility	*Quantity*	*Facility*	*Quantity*
Bank	1	Library	1
Castle	1	Municipal hall	1
Cemetery	1	Pub	1
Community hall	1	Restaurants	2
Health centre (unofficial; private house)	1	Veterinary centre	1
Hostel	1	Volunteer fire department	1
Joint water supply facility	1		

Branch of a Regional Cooperative Bank

days is characterized by small and even medium-scale industries as well as service offices. In the upper section of the village, former farming land was sold to various SMEs that have successfully established workshops and offices over there, providing jobs for a great part of the villagers. These manufacturers produce agricultural tools or animal food; some other companies provide marketing consulting, language translations or market research for products and services for senior villagers. There is also a car repair shop as well as a barber shop in Holzheim. Particularly outstanding is the biomedical technology company DiaSys, which employs more than 20 locals and operates — apart from its headquarters in Holzheim — several overseas distribution and research facilities and offices in Brazil, China, France, Japan and Russia, attracting many international clients and visitors to Holzheim. The company operates under the auspices of its subsidiary DiaWind a wind power plant on the upper hill area of the village, gainfully feeding the national power grid in the framework of Germany's renewable energy law.

Left Side: The Commercial Area of the Village

Other major employers are SMEs and public offices in the neighbouring cities of Limburg and Diez, thus the majority of Holzheim's working population are commercial employees and civil servants, followed by workers. There are several small scale companies and industries in the village, ranging from one-man enterprises to companies with over ten employees, engaging in sectors such as financial consulting, renewable energies, software design or professional photography. Witnessing the ongoing extinction of the former strongly agricultural character of Holzheim, now-a-days there

The Private Wind Power Station in Holzheim

Table 2.3: Industries and Companies in the Village

Medium scale industries	
1. Construction and mechanics based SSI	1
2. Medical based MSI	1
Small scale industries	
1. Construction and mechanics based SSI	4
2. Energy based SSI	2
3. Electronics based SSI	3
4. Food based SSI	3
5. Software based SSI	1
6. Textile based SSI	1
7. Other SSI	5
8. Agricultural enterprises/farms	3

are only three farmer families in the village. In terms of social standing or income, the population of Holzheim is quite homogeneous and there are no particularly rich or particularly poor people in the village. Most people live in their own three to four floor-houses and only few families live in apartments, clearly indicating a high standard of living in the village.

Communication Facilities

Holzheim is a very modern and technologically advanced German village. The coverage with electricity and landline phone connections is 100 per cent. Every household in the village possesses of electrical appliances such as televisions, stereo sound systems, washing machines, electric cookers, computers and many more. In 1980, the village was connected to the regional natural gas network providing citizens with access to gas for cooking and heating. Moreover, in 1985 Holzheim was the first municipality in the Rhein-Lahn-Kreis to be connected to the cable TV network of the Federal Post *via* satellite, which was followed by an enlargement of the broad band communication, TV and radio networks in Holzheim.[10] Since the early 2000s, the village is fully covered within Germany's broad band high speed internet network and more than 50 per cent of the villagers have internet connections in their homes and regularly use internet for work, communication and access to information.

Diagram 2.3: Structure of Village Administration and Governance Activities

NOTE: *Official Emblem of Holzheim: In the original, the darker part is in green colour.*

Local Governance Structure and Elections in Holzheim

As a municipality in the state of Rhineland-Palatinate, Holzheim as part of the AOM of Diez has both an Honorary Municipal Mayor (Ortsbürgermeister) as well as a Municipal Council (Ortsgemeinderat — MC), but not own offices for administration which are outsourced to Diez, executing administrative work in the name and behalf of Holzheim and other villages belonging to the AOM. There is only one local municipal worker in the village handling promulgation of programmes and assisting in the execution of the different programmes of the local village government. The municipal council is elected every five years in fair and secret elections by all villagers over 18 years of age and consists of twelve council members plus the (honorary) Municipal Mayor who has voting right.

Local elections in Holzheim are free and fair and enable the villagers to determine their representatives democratically. For decades elections were conducted by applying first-past-the-post-voting. First time in thirty-six years of Municipal Council's existence election was conducted by adopting proportional representation in June, 2009. This new method was adopted as the candidacy of many people had been failed miserably during the Assembly of eligible voters. Many who failed in this process, thus joined political parties or grouped themselves into two different Free Voters Groups (Freie Wählergruppe, FWG) in order to increase their chances. Thus, voting by proportional representation was introduced to Holzheim. One was the FWG-Meyer and the other one the FWG-Hillingshäuser. Also, members of the local branch of the Christian Democratic Union (CDU) joined the elections. The 2009 election results brought two members from one FWG, nine members of another FWG and one person from

Table 2.4: Results of 2009 Municipal Council Elections[11]

	FWG-M	*FWG-H*	*CDU*	*Total*
Votes	3462	727	501	4690
Percentage	73.8%	15.5%	10.7%	100%
Seats	9	2	1	12

the CDU to the council. The incumbent Mayor was reconfirmed in his office by 90.4 per cent of villagers.

Three members of the municipal council are women. There is absolutely no difference in equality of men and women in both the elective and administrative process of the local government. As the former village Mayor put it during the interview with the author: "People are elected, not genders". The incumbent mayor is head of one of the two remaining farming families in the villages and concurrently incumbent forester, responsible for Holzheim's forest area which is — along with the castle ruin Ardeck — under the jurisdiction of the local government. The village council meets every week in the municipal hall. The twelve municipal council members do not receive any financial compensation and carry out their duties thus on a voluntary basis. The Mayor receives a symbolical salary, which is, however, not sufficient to live on. People do these voluntary jobs thus not for monetary reasons, but rather out of pure dedication for the development of the village or sometimes also as a first step in a political career within a party. Some of the villagers are organized in those FWG, which

Table 2.5 : Municipal Council and Mayor of Holzheim

Name	*Sex*	*MC Position*	*Party*	*Votes in 2009 election*
Werner Dittmar*	Male	Hon. Mayor*	/	90.4% of votes*
Karl August Meyer	Male	MC Member	FWG-M	507
Gerhard Ohl	Male	MC Member	FWG-M	403
Alois Friedrich	Male	MC Member	FWG-M	359
Rainer Stahl	Male	MC Member	FWG-M	345
Klaus Langenau Jr.	Male	MC Member	FWG-M	321
Walter Meuer	Male	MC Member	FWG-M	263
Bernd Dietrich	Male	MC Member	FWG-M	235
Dagmar Link	Female	MC Member	FWG-M	228
Holger Nink	Male	MC Member	FWG-M	226
Ulrich Müller	Male	MC Member	FWG-H	205
Heidrun Schwenk	Female	MC Member	FWG-H	202
Klaus Birlenbach	Male	MC Member	CDU	119

are free associations of persons that take part in local elections without having the status of an officially registered political party. The FWGs of Holzheim have their own website and its policies and programmes are overwhelmingly geared to the local requirements and needs of the village, such as street infrastructure, waste management, environmental issue, youth programmes or promotion of cultural activities.

Performance of the Local Government

There are no legally binding functions or activities any village in the state of Rhineland-Palatinate is forced to carry out. The regular standard functions carried out by the local government can be classified into: (a) regular meetings of the village council and weekly visiting hours of the Mayor open to all villagers, (b) fostering the relationships with Holzheim's partner villages/communities in North Germany and Rwanda by annual excursions, and (c) festival functions organized by the local government. Firstly, there are annual "afternoon coffee functions" for the old villagers, which in fact are celebrative get-together in honour of Holzheim's senior villagers, where the local choirs perform songs. Secondly, there is an annual Christmas market in the village too, which however is not frequented by many villagers due to existing larger and better alternatives in the neighbouring cities.

The municipal Mayor and council envision a constantly harmonious and functioning village without quarrels and large social disparities. Particular attention is paid to supporting the local cultural associations and their operability. There currently two major future projects going on in the village: one is the so-called re-inauguration of the Aartalbahn in 2014, a revival of the local inter-village railway traffic through Diez. Another project is the heavily disputed construction of a by-

Right Side Front: The municipal hall of Holzheim, seat and meeting venue of the local administration. Left Side Back: The volunteer fire department

pass road — the so-called Südumgehung — from Limburg to Holzheim's neighbouring villages of Flacht and Niederneisen. Proponents and supporters of the road state its construction would very much help reduce traffic within Holzheim, which is connecting hub between Limburg, Diez and the villages of Flacht, Niederneisen, Hahnstätten, etc. Opponents and protestors, particularly constituted by the recently moved-in non-natives that live in the upper hillside part of Holzheim are afraid of noise disturbance and landscape destruction as this road would go across the green scenery and farming fields. This controversial topic has motivated local activists to stage protests and campaign for the village council in order to block any advancement of this construction projects. The controversy has also identified a split between many of the new Holzheimers and the native villagers which also tend to ridicule the arguments of the new villagers and despite their sense of competence as well as their lack of compassion in terms of the interests of the whole village, since this road project — being constructed vey distant from the village — would significantly improve village life and even security through relieving the currently heavy traffic flow.

For decades, there have not been direct party politics in the local body as most of the representatives have been doing their jobs mostly independently. Yet, this structure is in a process of change, not least by the engagement of the new villagers. There are few people with attachment to minor and large political parties (one of these the CDU). Some native villagers regard the coming up of party politics in the local governance body as disturbing in view of the interests of the village as people would rather campaign for their own interests and not for the interests of the village community as independent mayor and council members would do.

The incumbent mayor of Holzheim — one of the villagers who have nearly resided all their live over there — is currently confronted with a wide set of disputes with the council members, many of them people who recently settled in the village. Apart from topical conflicts of opinion — by summer 2011 there was much opposition against the planned enlargement of the development area — some members of the council harass the Mayor and his work by accusing him of procedural errors or demanding from him detailed preliminary explanation on agenda items before every council meeting, which is — in view of his only honorary function as Mayor and full-time workload as farmer and forester — criticized by many observant long-term villagers. Many villagers think that before 2009, local governance was more harmonious and successful.

Finances of the Local Administration[12]

For the 2009-2010 budget period, the balance of the municipal administration was :

Table 2.6: Income and Expenditure Details

		Amount
1.	**Profit and loss budget**	
	Total amount of income	1,440,082, - €
	Total amount of expenses	1,395,098, - €
	Net income / loss	44,984, - €
2.	**Cash-flow budget**	
	Ordinary deposits	952,208, - €
	Ordinary disbursements	1,244,363, - €
	Balance of ordinary deposits and withdrawals	–292,155, - €
	Extraordinary payments	25, - €
	Extraordinary payouts	0, - €
	Balance of outstanding deposits and withdrawals	25, - €
	Cash received from investment activities	124,100, - €
	Payoffs from investing activities	254,400, - €
	Balance of deposits and withdrawals from investment activities	–130,300, - €
	Cash received from financial activities	447,128, - €
	Disbursements from financing activities	24,698, - €
	Balance of deposits and withdrawals from financing activities	422,130, - €
	Total amount of deposits	1,523,461, - €
	Total amount of disbursements	1,523,461, - €
	Change in cash and cash equivalents during the financial year	0, - €
3.	**Planned loans**	
	Interest-bearing loans	71,928, - €

Taxes and Usage Fees

The small local village governmental body of Holzheim handles tax incomes of about 500,000 Euros per annum which are derived from land tax and corporate tax. Biggest tax payer in Holzheim is the local biomedical company. 75 per cent of the annual tax income — thus about 375,000 Euros — are transferred to the association of municipalities in form of taxes as well as compensation for handling the major bulk of the village's administrative work. The remaining money is employed on the one hand for the compensation of the mayor as well as the municipal worker, on the other hand for the maintenance of the public facilities, festival activities or infrastructural projects, such as building of new streets. The main sources of income available to the municipal administration can be classified into tax revenue and usage fees of public facilities.

The taxes and their rates are listed as follows :

(a) **Land Tax** – There are two types of land tax that are Land Tax A and Land Tax B. While the former is imposed on agricultural land, the latter is valid for plots of land for private estates. The rates are:
Land Tax A: 270%
Land Tax B: 320%

(b) **Corporate Tax** is 340 per cent

(c) **Dog Tax** – The tax on dogs kept within the region of the municipality. The rates are:
First dog: 40, - €
Second dog: 60, - €
Third and each additional dog: 80, - €
Fighting dogs: 320, - €

(d) **Fees and Contributions for Community Facilities** — The rates of fees and contributions for community facilities are based on the stipulations of the Municipal Tax Law of 20 June 1995. For the municipal hall (Aardeckhalle) they are structured as follows:

From the first date of use

- Entire hall with lounge, kitchen and its business operation : 280, - €
- Upper room including the kitchen : 120, - €
- Hall with business operations including the kitchen: 200, - €

- Hall without business operation including the kitchen : 180, - €
- Supplement for Floor protection : 100, - €

For each additional day

- Entire hall with lounge, kitchen and its business operation : 220, - €
- Upper common room including the kitchen: 80, €
- Hall with business operations including the kitchen : 160, - €
- Hall without business operation including the kitchen : 140, - €

The fees include costs for cleaning. If a staff member of the community is needed, the organizers are liable to these costs. With external users and for commercial events, a special agreement is to be concluded.

(e) **Other** – The unit rate per square metre of land drained for the construction work carried out is set to 12.82€.

Equity Holdings

Holzheim is one of the few municipalities in Germany which is not in debts but even generates surpluses, allowing for the retaining of capital for larger projects:

Expected level of equity as of 01 January 2009	: 4,442,717.12
Expected level of equity as of 31 December 2009	: 4,487,701.12

Innovative Activities

Domestic and International Partnerships: A Cornerstone of the Village

A particular important aspect of the village is its active partnerships with other villages and communities around the world. Holzheim has communal partnerships with Mönkeberg in Northern Germany and the sector of Rambura in the African country Rwanda. In 20 July 1988, the local municipality Holzheim concluded a partnership agreement with the municipality Giciye in Sector Birembo in Rwanda, which after an administrative reform became Rambura in the district of Nyabhihu in the country's Western Province. This village-level partnership came into existence along with the partnership framework between the state of Rhineland-Palatinate and the Republic of Rwanda in Central Africa, established by the former State Chief Minister Bernhard Vogel. This partnership between a federal state and a country is unique throughout Germany and has been lauded by all political colours in the country, lately by the former German President and Africa enthusiast Horst Köhler. Holzheim's partnership with a sector in Rwanda has been initiated, promoted and actively fostered by nearly annual visits by the former municipal Mayor Helmut Weimar, who after his retirement of serving 25 years as Mayor in 2004 became official Delegate of Rwandan Affairs of Holzheim and since then continues with other local enthusiasts to support the reconstruction and development of the village's African partner community. In 2006, he was awarded the Federal Cross of Merit for his lifelong engagement and work for this communal partnership.

This partnership for nearly 25 years helped for the construction of a primary school for more than 900 children, health centres, over 122 natural fountains ensuring the provision with drinking water, a vocational training school and many many more things.[13] Annually, the Delegate for Rwandan affairs and other villagers of Holzheim travel together to Rwanda to visit the funded projects and consult with the locals about new projects. The visits always result in large welcome ceremonies of the partner community to honour the visitors and their huge and long-term help and commitment to their development. Holzheim is the smallest village in the state of Rhineland-Palatinate that has a partnership with a commune in the Third World. Holzheim has, therefore, become one of the very few United Nations (UN) Millennium Municipalities in the framework of the UN Millennium Programmes against poverty.

Former Mayor of Holzheim and the Delegate of Rwandan Affairs of Holzheim, Helmut Weimar, in a crowd of young students in the partner district Rambura, Rwanda

The partnership with Mönkeberg was established in 1984 and has been strengthened by numerous mutual visits between villagers and officials of the two municipalities in the over 25 years of partnership. Particularly remarkable was the inauguration of a fountain by representatives of the two municipalities in 1990 in Holzheim, when the band of Mönkeberg accompanied the inauguration musically.[14]

Cultural and Livelihood Engagement of the People

Festival, Functions and Social Activities

Holzheim is a village abundant in various cultural functions that enrich village life. Apart from German traditional family conventions during Christmas, the most important religious and cultural festival in Germany celebrated from 24 to 26 December each year with the first day being the most important one where family members sit and dine together and many of them (Protestants) attending the evening Mass at the church in the neighbouring village Flacht, as well as Easter — celebrated annually between March and April — which is particularly celebrated by the predominantly (over 80%) catholic population of Holzheim.

There are many more social functions that have become more and more a typical appearance in the village. One of these are the barbecue parties in warm summer days, when many villagers invite family members, friends and neighbours to come their houses, sit together in the garden and eat, drink and chat. In addition to this and season-independent there are various get together events and coffee afternoons among neighbours and best friends. Like in most German cities, townships and villages, the birth of new son or daughter is also celebrated with a so called "Baby Party". In Holzheim, there is much social interaction and communal activities, but the majority of them takes place in private circles or neighbourhoods were people know each other for long time. It is, therefore, that new people in the neighbourhood do not easily find access to these functions and normally require the invitation by one member of the "social circle" in order to participate and exchange with the sworn community. In Germany, one usually refrains from uninvited show ups.

Livelihood Activities — Local Clubs and Associations

The livelihood activities of the villagers are manifold, yet in Holzheim activities through any sort of association and club are considered an integral part of community life and social interaction. These cover two theatre societies, three choral societies, two dance groups, one horticultural society and one women's group, the latter being a discussion forum. One of these theatre societies organizes every two years a play at the coulisse setting of the Ardeck castle. These plays are quite famous in Germany and attract visitors from many different parts of the country and even international guests. The stories of the comedian plays are normally settled in pre-modern Holzheim make heavy use of local dialect and idioms. There is also a voluntary fire brigade in Holzheim where youth from young age can participate and learn every aspects of fire fighting. Holzheim also has a handball club — founded in 1888 — that is trans-regionally successful and has a considerable reputation in the regional handball scene. Most young people in Holzheim join any of these associations and in doing so also foster ties and social interaction with their peers.

Current Conflicts

The main current conflict is that of the construction of the by-pass road that partly splits the new villagers in the development areas of the upper hillside of Holzheim and the long-term residents, which has already left traces in the local government as already mentioned. Although there is real intention by several new villagers to integrate well into traditional community life of Holzheim through various associations, clubs and events, there are still some villagers with reservations against these people, be it for diverging political opinions or socio-communal reasons of distinguishing between "real" natives and new non-natives. Another big share of conflicts are those between neighbours. Some of these conflicts have long historic roots of personal disliking, while others are a result of issues such as tree sizes, car parking, street cleaning, etc. For these minor conflicts, Holzheim has an honorary arbitrator — currently the former long-term Mayor and current chargé of Rwandan affairs — who in his capacity as credible and neutral person among the villagers seeks to moderate and conciliate between quarrelling neighbours before they put their disputes a step further to the courts, where conflicts start to become more severe and cost money.

Concluding Remarks

The regulation about local self-administration in the state of Rhineland-Palatinate provides residents of villages with a comparably high degree of creative power to decide the handling of local affairs. Every five years, free and fair elections to the municipal council enable the villagers to determine the composition of their local representatives and, with regard to the disputed project Südumgehung, the current MC also resembles democratically the current conflict line and political positions within the village. The MC decides itself on the necessity and execution of projects taking into consideration the interests of the village and its residents. Although execution of administrative work may — due to it being outsourced to the AOM — sometimes experience small delays, the handling of Holzheim's administrative issues by the AOM of Diez usually is without major problems.

A particularly important issue is the preservation of Holzheim's idyllic and green appearance for which environmental issues in terms of regulated tree-cutting, waste collection or settling of industries are constantly discussed and updated to adapt to both environmental requirements and the needs of the villagers. Apart from this, the village administration engages much in cultural and caretaking activities for its villagers, particularly the aged generation. A similar concern is also the preservation of its cultural heritage. Holzheim's administration can thus be characterized as environmental-friendly, culturally preserving and pro-aged people.

Although there are no particular programmes by the MC to combat poverty — since poverty is not a striking issue in Holzheim at all — the village can in view of its voluntary, yet very strong engagement and partnership in Africa nevertheless be characterized as very pro-poor, to a degree that there are regular festival activities with many villagers organizing and conducting them free of salary except for demanding contributions for development aid in the partner sector. Moreover, some villagers regularly fly to the country on their own expenses to supervise the *status quo* of their projects. In a sum, Holzheim is a unique village in Germany with a strong local administration. The village is in view of the size of its populace very abundant in activities and projects that keep on improving livelihood in Holzheim.

REFERENCES

1. Tilkorn (2004), p. 7.
2. *Ibid.*, pp. 7–8.
3. *Ibid.*, p. 11.
4. Ministry of Justice and Consumer Protection of Rhineland-Palatinate (2011).
5. 1 Morgen equates to 36 Ar.
6. Cited from Charter 3135 of the Lorsch Codex. University of Erlangen (n.d.).
7. Landesregierung Rheinland-Pfalz: Generaldirektion Kulturelles Erbe (2010), p. 27.
8. Orsgemeinde Holzheim (2011).
9. Statistical Office of Rhineland-Palatinate (2011), p. 26.
10. Schughart/Theis (1995), p. 280.
11. Orsgemeinde Holzheim (2009).
12. http://www.holzheim.net/aus%20dem%20Gemeinderat/332-haushaltssatzung-der-gemeinde-holzheim-fuer-das-jahr-2009-vom-07042009.html
13. Schughart/Theis (1995), p. 273.
14. *Ibid.*, p. 280.

NOTES

Gensike, Hellmuth/ Heck, Hermann (1972), 1200 Jahre Holzheim. Beiträge zur 1200 jährigen Geschichte des Dorfes [1,200 years Holzheim. Contributions to the 1,200-year history of the village]. Holzheim: Ortsgemeinde Holzheim.

Landesregierung Rheinland-Pfalz: Generaldirektion Kulturelles Erbe [State government of Rhineland-Palatinate: Directorate General for Cultural Heritage] (2010), *Nachrichtliches Verzeichnis der Kulturdenkmäler: Rhein-Lahn-Kreis* [Memorandum list of cultural monuments: Rhein-Lahn District], 1 October. Online: http://denkmallisten.gdke-rlp.de/Rhein-Lahn-Kreis.pdf (accessed: 29 September 2011).

Ministry of Justice and Consumer Protection of Rhineland-Palatinate (2011), Gemeindeordnung (GemO) in der Fassung vom 31. January 1994. Online: http://landesrecht.rlp.de/jportal/portal/t/218o/page/bsrlpprod.psml/action/portlets.jw.MainAction?p1=2r&eventSubmit_do Navigate=searchInSubtreeTOC&showdoccase=1&doc. hl=0&doc.id=jlr-GemORPV14P68&doc.part=S&toc. poskey=#focuspoint (accessed: 27 September 2011).

Ortsgemeinde Holzheim [Holzheim Municipality] (2009), *Artikel in der NNP zum Wahlergebnis* [Articles in the NNP regarding the election results], 9 June. Online: http://www.holzheim.net/alle-bekanntmachungen/53-kommunalwahl-07062009/358-artikel-in-der-nnp-zum-wahlergebnis.html (accessed: 30 October 2011).

Ortsgemeinde Holzheim [Holzheim Municipality] (2011), *Burg Ardeck: Bewohner bis 1727* [Ardeck Castle: inhabitants up to 1727]. Online: http://holzheim.net/kultur/burgruine-ardeck/Bewohner%20bis%201727.html (accessed: 14 September 2011).

Schughart, Karl and Theis, Friedhelm (1995), *Holzheim und seine Burg — 600 Jahre Burg Ardeck 1395 — 1995* [Holzheim and her castle — 600 years of Ardeck castle 1395–1995]. Holzheim: Gemeinde Holzheim.

Schwenk, Dieter (2007), *Überseeische Auswanderung im 19. Jahrhundert* [Overseas emigration in the 19th century]. Online: http://holzheim.net/kultur/auswanderer -aus-holzheim.html, Updated: 22 September (accessed: 18 September 2011).

Statistisches Landesamt Rheinland-Pfalz [Statistical Office of Rhineland-Palatinate] (2011), *Statistische Berichte: Bevölkerung der Gemeinden am 31. Dezember 2010* [Statistical reports: population in the municipalities as of 31 December 2010]. Online: http://www.statistik.rlp.de/fileadmin/dokumente/berichte/A1033_201022_hj_G.pdf (accessed: 31 October 2011).

Tilkorn, Erich (2004), 'Local Self-Government in Germany. An Outline', in: Friedrich Ebert Stiftung.Online:http://www.fes.hr/

Ebooks/pdf/Reforming%20Local%2 Public%20 Administration/02.pdf (accessed: 27 September 2011), pp. 7-15.

University of Erlangen (n.d.), *Urkunde 3135 aus dem Lorschen Kodex* [Document 3135 from the LorschCodex].Online:http:/ /www8.informatik.unierlangen.de/cgiin/stoyan/urkunde/ NO=3135/BASE=Lorsch (accessed: 26 September 2011).

Chapter III

Rural Local Governance in India

PART 1

Manipur: An Overview

Manipur, the easternmost part of India is an isolated hill girt State extending from 93° 03' to 94° 47' east longitudes and 23° 50' north to 25° 40' North latitudes. Nagaland borders it on the north on the east by Myanmar, on the south partly by Mizoram and the Chin hills of Myanmar, and on the west by Cachar district of Assam. The total area of the State is 22,356 sq. km. Manipur hills provide the geographical base of the State as they cover about 90 per cent of its area surrounding the small central valley accommodating over one-third of the population of the State. The hills comprise five tribal districts: Senapati, Tamenglong, Churachandpur, Ukhrul, and Chandel.

Social-cultural pluralism is the core of the social fabric of Manipur. The State consisted of three major ethnic groups. The 'Meitei' (Manipur Hindus), 'Naga', and "Kukichin' (both tribal groups) with various migrant communities and the 'Pangal' (Manipur Muslims). The Meiteis were converted to Hinduism and accepted the caste system while the Nagas and Kukichin groups were converted into Christianity. The Muslim

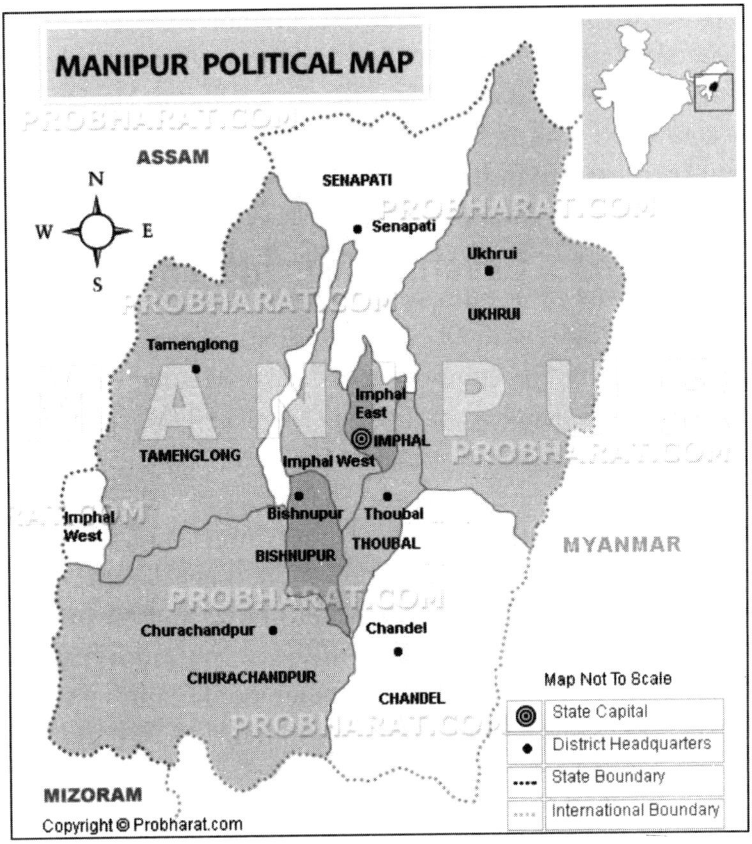

Map 3.1: Map of Manipur

community while accepting Meitei language constitutes a distinct social and cultural group based on religious profession.

Background of Imphal East District

Imphal East District came into existence on 18.06.1997 with its headquarters at Porompat occupying the eastern part of Imphal District. The District is situated in two separate valleys of the State namely Central Valley and Jiribam Valley. The total area of the District is 469.44 sq. km approximately. It has no rail network and hence, communication is entirely dependent on roads except Jiribam Sub-Division bordering Cachar District of Assam where there is a railhead. The District is connected with N.H. 39, N.H. 53 and N.H. 150.

There are four Revenue Sub-Divisions in the district namely: (1) Porompat Sub-Division; (2) Sawombung Sub-Division; (3) Keirao Bitra Sub-Division, and (4) Jiribam Sub-Division. The total number of SDC Revenue Circles in the district is 9 (nine) with 237 revenue villages. There are 4 (four) Urban Local Bodies comprising of 2 (two) Municipalities and 2 (two) Nagar Panchayats. The two Municipalities are Imphal Municipal Council and Jiribam Municipal Council whereas; the two Nagar Panchayats are Andro Nagar Panchayat and Lamlai Nagar Panchayat. There are 3 (three) C.D. Blocks in the district namely: (1) Imphal East-I C.D. Block, Sawombung; (2) Imphal East-II C.D. Block, Keirao Bitra; and (3) Jiribam C.D. Block, Jiribam. Altogether, there are 56 (fifty-six) Gram Panchayats in the district. Block-wise distributions of Gram Panchayats are given in Table 3.1.

Table 3.1: Block-wise Distributions of Zilla Parishad/Gram Panchayats/Gram Panchayat Member and Population in Imphal East District

Sl. No.	*Name of Community Development (CD) Block*	*No. of ZP Members*	*No. of GP*	*No. of GP Member*	*Population (1991 Census)*
1.	Imphal East-I CD Block, Sawombung	9	25	226	1,13,508
2.	Imphal East-II CD) Block, Keirao Bitra	8	25	206	1,13,059
3.	Jiribam CD Block, Jiribam	2	6	56	28,077
	Total	19	56	488	2,54,644

The total number of Assembly segments in the district is 11 (eleven). They are (1) Khundrakpam A.C.; (2) Heingang A.C.; (3) Khurai A.C.; (4) Kshetrigao A.C.; (5) Thongju A.C.;

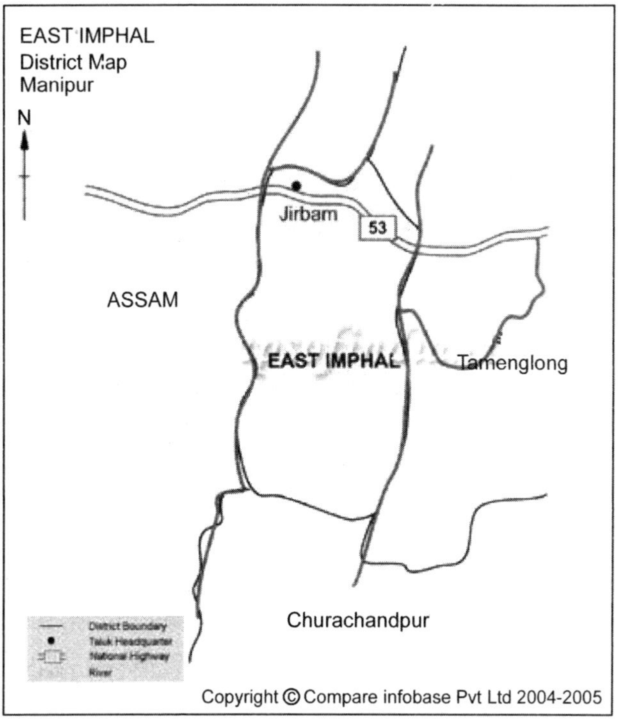

Map 3.2: Map of Imphal East District

(6) Keirao A.C.; (7) Andro A.C.; (8) Lamlai A.C.; (9) Yaiskul A.C.; (10) Wangkhei A.C.; and (11) Jiribam A.C.

Khundrakpam A.C. consists of 37 (thirty-seven) Villages, Heingang A.C. consists of 20 (twenty) villages, Khurai A.C. consists of 17 (seventeen) villages, Kshetrigao A.C. consists of 11 (eleven) villages, Thongju A.C. consists of 10 (ten) villages, Keirao A.C. consists of 12 (twelve) villages, Andro A.C. consists of 13 (thirteen) villages, Lamlai A.C. consists of 41 (forty one) villages, Yaiskul A.C. consists of 3 (three) villages, Wangkhei A.C. consists of 5 (five) villages, and Jiribam A.C. consists of 60 (sixty) villages.

The population of the District is 2,54,644 according to 1991 census. The rural population is 77.06 per cent whereas the urban population of the district is 22.94 per cent. Male population is 1,68,125 whereas female population of the district is 1,62,335. The population of the Scheduled Castes in the district is 3.98 per cent of the total population of the district. The population of Scheduled Tribes in the district is 5.81 per cent of the total population of the district. Literacy rate of the district is 68.05 per cent as per 1991 Census.

Local Governance Framework in Manipur

The present Panchayat system in Manipur was introduced in 1960. In the year 1960, the United Province Panchayati Raj Act 1947 (U.P. Act No. 26 of 1947) was extended to the State of Manipur (than in the status of Union Territory) excluding the Hill areas, municipal areas, cantonment areas and notified areas. Under the Act, a two-tier system of Panchayats was established in the Manipur valley and Jiribam area. Necessary rules were framed in 1962 for making applicable the various provisions of the Act.

Under the Uttar Pradesh Panchayati Raj Act and the rules framed thereunder, the first General Election was held in the year 1962 wherein 227 Gram Panchayats and 43 Nyaya Panchayats were constituted. The number of these institutions increased to 221 and 44 respectively after the second General Elections to Panchayats, held in the year 1970.

After the attainment of statehood by Manipur in 1972, the State government enacted the Manipur Panchayati Raj Act 1975, which provided for a three-tier system of Panchayats in the State comprising Gram Panchayats at the village level, Panchayat Samitis at the Block level and Zilla Parishad at the district level, besides Nyaya Panchayats for judicial purposes (Singh, R.P. and Lal Dena, 2006:261). The Manipur Panchayati Raj Act came into effect from 9th May, 1975 and became operative from 10th January 1978. Under this Act, 107 Gram Panchayats; 37 Nyaya Panchayats; and 6 Panchayat Samitis were established and the third general election was held in May 1978 ushering in the era of two-tier system of Panchayati Raj. The fourth General Election was held in 1985 pursuant to which 166 Gram Panchayats, 42 Nyaya Panchayats and 9 Panchayat Samitis were constituted. The fifth general election to the Panchayats was held in 1991.

Post-73rd Constitutional Amendment Development

Pursuant to the 73rd Constitutional Amendment providing Panchayats a constitutional status, Government of Manipur enacted the Manipur Panchayati Raj Act 1994 which came into force from 23rd April 1994 extending to all parts of the State barring the areas to which the District Council Act 1971 or the Manipur Village Authorities in Hill Areas Act 1956 was applicable.

The changed structure created again a two-tier system but deviating from the past, Zilla Parishad at the district level and the Village Panchayats at the village level. The elections for Panchayati Raj bodies were held towards the end of January 1997 paving for the creation of 166 Gram Panchayats and 3 Zilla Parishads, viz., Imphal, Thoubal and Bishnupur in March 1997. The Imphal Zilla Parishad was bifurcated into two, i.e., Imphal East and Imphal West in October 1997.

Out of the total area of 23,327 sq. km of the State, the area under Panchayati Raj Institutions was only 2,100 sq. km forming the rural tracts in the valley districts including Jiribam area. On an average, a Gram Panchayat covered an area of 12.65 sq. km, the Nyaya Panchayat 50 sq. km, and the Panchayat Samiti 233. 33 sq. km.

Diagram 3.1 : Panchayati Raj Set-Ups (Organizational Chart) Manipur

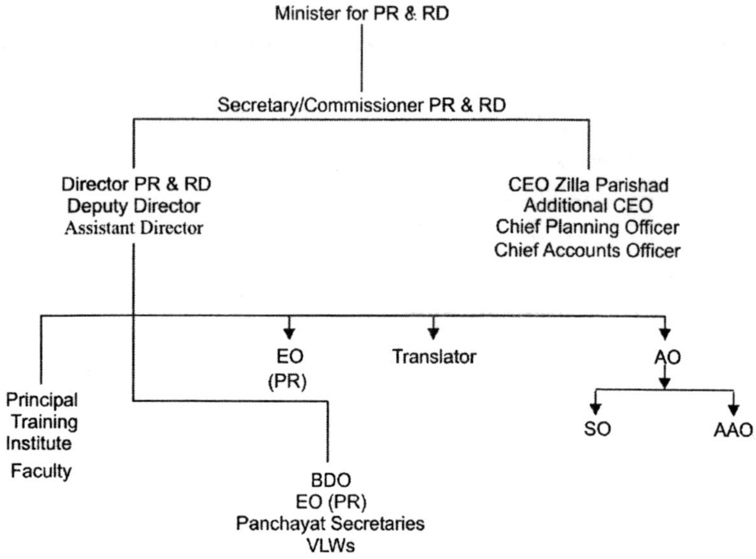

At present, there are 4 Zilla Parishads, 9 CD (Community Development) Blocks and 166 Gram Panchayats distributed across the four valley Districts of Manipur. For administrative convenience each of the four districts are sub-divided into Community Development Blocks. Thus, Imphal West District with one Zilla Parishad is divided into 2 CD Blocks, *viz.*, Imphal West-I CD Block consisting of 29 GPs and Imphal West-II CD Block consisting of 15 GPs; Imphal East District has three CD Blocks, viz., Imphal East-I CD Block with 25 GPs, Imphal East-II CD Block with another 25 GPs and Jiribam CD Block with 6 GPs; Thoubal District has 2 CD Blocks, *viz.*, Thoubal CD Block with 27 GPs and Kakching CD Block with 15 GPs; and Bishnupur District has 2 CD Blocks, *viz.*, Bishnupur C.D. Block with 12 GPs and Moirang C.D. Block with another 12 GPs. District-wise distribution of Panchayati Raj bodies is given in Table 3.2.

Table 3.2: District-wise Distribution of Panchayati Raj Bodies in Manipur

Sl. No.	*District*	*No. of Zilla Parishad*	*No. of Blocks*	*No. of Gram Panchayat*
1.	Imphal West District	1	2	44
2.	Imphal East District	1	3	56
3.	Thoubal District	1	2	42
4.	Bishnupur District	1	2	24
	Total	4	9	166

Governor

Chief Minister

Minister for PR & RD

Zilla Parishad Adhyaksha

Zilla UP Adhyaksha Members

Pradhans of Gram Panchayat

Vice Pradhan

Members of G.P.

Diagram 3.2: Administrative hierarchy of Panchayati Raj Set – ups

Village Administration in Manipur

The Manipur Panchayati Raj Act 1994 provides for a two-tier system of local government in Manipur, i.e., Zilla Parishad at the district level and Gram Panchayat at the village level.

Gram Sabha : Its Composition and Membership

Section 3(1) of the Manipur Panchayati Raj Act 1994 provides for the Constitution of Gram Sabha consisting of all the villagers whose names are included in the electoral roll of the Manipur Legislative Assembly. However, no person shall be a member of more than one Gram Sabha.[1] A member of Gram Sabha shall cease to be a member if he ceases to reside ordinarily within the Gram Sabha areas. On such cessation, he shall also cease to hold any office, which he held on election or appointment by virtue of his being a member of his Gram Sabha.[2]

Powers and Functions of Gram Sabha

A Gram Sabha shall meet from time to time but six months shall not intervene between the two meetings.[3] The Gram Sabha will have the power to discuss the agenda prepared by the concerned Gram Panchayat in relation to these matters, *viz.*, (a) The annual statement of accounts of the Gram Panchayat, the report of administration of the preceding financial year and the last audit note and reply, if any, made thereto; (b) The budget of the Gram Panchayat for the next financial year, and (c) The report in respect of development programmes proposed to be undertaken during the current year.[4]

The Gram Sabha may also form one or more Vigilance Committee consisting of persons who are not members of the Gram Panchayat, to supervise the Gram Panchayat works, schemes and other activities and put up reports concerning them in its meeting.[5]

Gram Panchayat : Its Election and Terms

Every Gram Sabha has its own Gram Panchayat. A Gram Panchayat shall consist of a Pradhan and an Up-Pradhan and such number of directly elected members as may be notified by the Government of Manipur from time to time. Seats shall be reserved for SCs and STs in every Gram Panchayat and such seats shall be allotted by rotation to different constituencies in such Gram Panchayat, in such a manner as may be prescribed. Not less than one-third of the total number of seats reserved for SCs and STs shall be reserved for their women. Not less than one-third (including the number of seats reserved for SC and ST women) of the total number as seats to be filled by direct election in every Gram Panchayat shall be reserved for women and such seats may be allotted by rotation to different constituencies in a Gram Panchayat in such a manner as may be prescribed. The term of Gram Panchayat is five years from the date of its first meeting. The election to constitute a Gram Panchayat shall be completed before the expiration of its term and in the case of dissolution, before the expiration of six months from the date of its dissolution. However, a Gram Panchayat reconstituted after its dissolution shall continue only for the remainder.[6]

Powers and Functions of Gram Panchayat

Administrative Functions[7]

A Gram Panchayat shall discharge the following administrative functions :

General functions, such as, preparation of annual plans for the development of the Panchayat area; Preparation of annual budget; Mobilization of reliefs in natural calamities; Removal of encroachments on public properties; Organization of voluntary labour and contribution for community works; Maintenance of essential statistics of village and so on. Agriculture including Agriculture Extension; Animal husbandry, Dairying and Poultry; Development of Fisheries in the villages; Social and Farm Forestry, Minor Forest produce; Fuel and Fodder; Khadi, Village and Cottage

Industries; Rural Housing; Drinking Water; Roads, buildings, culverts, bridges, ferries, waterways and other means of communication; Non-conventional energy source; Poverty Alleviation Programme; Education including primary schools and secondary schools; Promotion of Adult literacy; Village libraries and reading rooms; Promotion of social and cultural activities; Regulation of fairs (including cattle fairs) and festivals; Rural Sanitation such as; Public health and family welfare; Woman and child; Social welfare including welfare of the handicapped and mentally retarded; Welfare of the weaker section; Public distribution system; Maintenance of community assets; Construction and maintenance of Dharmashala, chatras and similar other institutions; Construction and maintenance of cattle sheds, pounds and cart stands; Construction and maintenance of slaughterhouses; Maintenance of public parks, playgrounds; Regulation of manure pits in public places; Establishment and control of Sandies; Irrigation, water management and watershed development; Rural electrification including distribution of electricity; Management and maintenance of forest situated in the Panchayat area; Management of wastelands, pasture lands or vacant lands belonging to the Government of Manipur situated within the Panchayat area; Collection of land revenue and maintenance of records connected therewith; and Any other functions as transferred/entrusted to the Gram Panchayat with its concurrence by the Government of Manipur.[8]

Power of Taxation[9]

A Gram Panchayat shall have the power to impose yearly tax on lands and building situated within its local jurisdiction, but subject to such rules as may be made in this respect. Subject to such, maximum rates as may be prescribed by the

Government of Manipur, a Gram Panchayat may levy within its local limits (a) a fee for providing sanitary services at the places of worship and pilgrimage, fairs and melas; (b) a rate for lighting is made by the Panchayat; and (c) a conservancy rate where arrangement for cleaning private latrines, urinals and cesspools is made by the Panchayat.

Zilla Parishad : Its Composition, Election, Members and Term

A district shall have a district level Panchayati body, *viz.*, Zilla Parishad. A Zilla Parishad consists of (a) members directly elected from its territorial constituencies; (b) members of the Lok Sabha and members of the Manipur Legislative Assembly whose respective constituencies partly or wholly fall within the local limits of the Zilla Parishad, i.e., the district for which it is established; and (c) 10 per cent of the Pradhans of the Gram Panchayat established/constituted within the district. But if the total number of the Lok Sabha members and Manipur Legislative Assembly members and Pradhan members exceed the total number of directly elected members, then only one-third of Pradhan members shall be selected on rotation for one year by lots as the Government of Manipur may decide from time to time and district to district. A Pradhan member so selected shall not be eligible for selection for the second term during the same term of his office as a Pradhan. All the members of the Zilla Parishad whether elected or not shall have the right to vote in all its meetings except in the election of its Adhyaksha and Up-Adhyaksha.[10] Seats shall be reserved for (a) the Scheduled Castes; and (b) the Scheduled Tribes. At least one-third of these reserved seats shall be reserved for Scheduled Caste and Scheduled Tribe women. Besides, at least one-third (including the seats reserved for SC/ST women) of the total seats to be filled by direct election in every Zilla Parishad shall be reserved to different constituencies in a Zilla Parishad, in such manner as may be prescribed.[11]

The term of a Zilla Parishad is five years from the date of its first meeting. Election shall be held to constitute a Zilla Parishad before the expiry of its term and in case of dissolution, before the expiry of six months from the date of its dissolution.[12]

Powers and Functions of Zilla Parishad

A Zilla Parishad exercises the following powers and functions: (i) Administrative functions, (ii) General functions, (iii) Financial power, (iv) Power of taxation, and (v) Power to make regulations.

Administrative Functions[13]

A Zilla Parishad shall discharge the following administrative functions:

Agriculture and Agriculture Extension; Irrigation of ground water resources and watershed Development; Horticulture; Statistics; Distribution of essential commodities; Soil Conservation and land reforms; Marketing; Social forestry; Animal Husbandry and Dairying; Minor forest product, Fuel and fodder; Fisheries; Household Industries (including food processing); Rural Roads and Inland water-ways; Health and Hygiene; Rural Housing; Education; Social Welfare and Welfare of weaker Sections and Handicapped persons; Poverty Alleviation programmes; Drinking Water; Rural Electrification; Non-conventional Energy Sources; Social Reform Activities; Undertaking and execution of any development scheme jointly with the Zilla Parishad of the adjacent district under agreement; Execution of any other function transferred to it (i.e., Zilla Parishad) by the Government of Manipur); Preparation of annual development plan of the district after including the development plans of the Gram Panchayats within its jurisdiction and submission of the same to the District Planning Committee.[14]

General Functions[15]

A Zilla Parishad may (a) sanction expenditure on educational or medical relief outside its local limits; (b) carry out any work, which would permit the welfare of the inhabitants of the district; (c) contribute to the association of all India, State or Inter-State level concerned with the promotion of local government and hold exhibition, seminars and conference within the district in relation to the activities of Gram Panchayat and Zilla Parishad; (d) render financial or other assistance to any activities carrying out in the district which is related to any of the function of the Zilla Parishad; and (e) do all the acts necessary for the due exercise of its powers and functions under the Act.

A Zilla Parishad also has the power to do the work signed to it by the Government of Manipur or the work assigned by the Central Government to the Government of Manipur.[16]

Financial Power[17]

A Zilla Parishad may (a) raise from time to time, with the approval of the Government of Manipur, loans for the due discharge of its powers and functions under the Act and create a sinking fund for the repayment of such loans; and (b) borrow money from the Government of Manipur, from banks or other financial institutions for the performance of the schemes drawn up by it (Zilla Parishad). A Zilla Parishad shall also have the power to prepare its own budget for the following year and shall submit the same to the Government of Manipur for approval. The Government may either approve the budget or return it to the Zilla Parishad for modifications. On modification being made, the Zilla Parishad shall resubmit the budget to the Government for its approval and if the Zilla Parishad does not receive the approval by the last date of the financial year, the budget shall be deemed to be approved by the Government. A Zilla Parishad shall not, however, incur any expenditure unless its budget is approved by the Government of Manipur.[18]

A Zilla Parishad shall maintain its account in the prescribed manner and the account shall be audited by the authority prescribed by the Government of Manipur.[19]

Power of Taxation[20]

A Zilla Parishad may levy (a) tolls on persons, vehicles or animals or any class of them at any toll-bar established by it on any road except kutcha road or any bridge vested in it or under its managements; (b) tolls in respect of any ferry established by it or under its management; (c) road cess and public work cess; (d) fees on the registration of boats or vehicle, on sanitary facilities at such places, pilgrims, fairs and melas within its jurisdiction as may be notified by the Government of Manipur, on licence for fair or mela and rates of lighting of streets/places and supply of water. However, the levy of these tolls, fees, cess, rates and so on, shall not exceed the maximum rates prescribed by the Government of Manipur and the scales, terms and conditions of such tolls, fees, cess, rates, etc., shall be regulated by the Government of Manipur.

Power to make Regulations[21]

A Zilla Parishad may make regulations to carry out its powers and functions under the Act, but the making of the regulations shall be (a) by notification; (b) subject to the provisions of the Act and the rules framed thereunder; (c) with the previous sanction of the Government of Manipur; and (d) subject to the previous publication in the prescribed manner.

District Planning Committee[22]

The Government of Manipur shall constitute for every district a District Planning Committee to consolidate the plans prepared by the Zilla Parishad, Gram Panchayat, Nagar Panchayat, Municipal Council and Municipal Corporation in the district and to prepare a draft development plan for the district as a whole. The District Planning Committee shall consist of (a) Members of the Lok Sabha whose respective Constituencies partly or wholly fall within the district; (b) Members of the Manipur Legislative Assembly whose respective Constituencies partly or wholly fall within the district; (c) Adhyaksha of Zilla Parishad; (d) Mayor or President of the Municipal Corporation or the Municipal Council respectively having jurisdiction over the headquarters of the District; (e) Members elected in the prescribed manner from amongst the members of the Zilla Parishad, Nagar Panchayat and Councillors of the Municipal Corporation and the Municipal Councils in the district (up to fourth-fifth of the total number of the Committee's members) and the election must maintain proportionate ratio between the population of the rural areas and that of the urban areas in the district; (f) Chairman of the District Co-operative Banks and the Land Development Banks as permanent invitees; (g) Chief Executive

Officer of the Zilla Parishad as the Secretary of the Committee; and (h) Deputy Commissioner of the District as Chairman of the Committee.

The District Planning Committee shall consolidate the plans prepared by the Zilla Parishad, Gram Panchayat, Nagar Panchayat, Municipal Council and Municipal Corporation in the district and prepare a draft development plan for the district as a whole. The Chairman of the District Planning Committee shall forward the development plan, as recommended by the Committee, to the Government of Manipur.

PART II

Local Governance in Action — Manipur

Tellou Channa Seijang Gram Panchayat

Tellou Channa Seijang Gram Panchayat is the largest of the 25 Gram Panchayats in Imphal East-I Sawombung Block. It is located 35 km away from the Block headquarters of Imphal East-I and 37 km away from the capital city of Manipur. It covers 18 small and medium size villages over an area of nearly 5,700 hectares in a rural setting with the population of 5,720 (2001). The Scheduled Castes population was 46 per cent and general castes were 44 per cent. The literacy percentage of the GP was 35 per cent (25% male and 10% female). Agriculture and petty was the prime income sources of the people.

Powers of Panchayat : Assessment of Ground Reality

Tellou Channa Seijang Gram Panchayat enjoys none of the

functions constitutionally mandated to it by the Manipur Panchayati Raj Act 1994. By and large, it remains only an implementing agency of the Central as well as State-sponsored Schemes in the State. At the most it is empowered with identification of beneficiaries and distributions of Job-Cards for MREGA (Manipur Rural Employment Guarantee Act). Line departments often undertake functions mandated to the Panchayats. In Tellou Channa Seijang Gram Panchayat, Zilla Parishad often undertakes functions mandated to the Gram Panchayat. Gram Panchayats and Zilla Parishads have been empowered under the Manipur Panchayati Raj Act 1994 to levy toll, cess and fees to mobilize their own resources. However, in reality, the ZPs and GPs do not levy any taxes, fees, etc. Funds, notably PMGSY and MREGS dominated the scene of Panchayat finance. Under such a situation, little autonomous functioning of the Panchayat could be expected.

Existing Capacity of Gram Sabha

So much hype has been created around the possible virtues of the Gram Sabha in the post-73rd Amendment phase that any discussion on the failure of the Panchayats ultimately boils down to the dysfunctional Gram Sabha. In fact all these perceived failures of Panchayats are attributed to the fact that people do not stand anywhere in the whole scheme of decentralization.

Why do people not participate in the activities of the Panchayats? Is it true that Panchayat leaders do not wish to encourage the people to participate in the activities of the local level institutions? Alternatively, is it equally true that people are prompted by selfish motives, displaying a total disregard for civic life — in short, too self-centred and apathetic to the whole idea of decentralization, which, paradoxically, revolves around the people themselves? Or is there a serious flaw with the basic construct of this institution and its functional domain? The inhibiting factors could be many. However, the oft-repeated cliché is that people do not attend Gram Sabha meetings. To assess the ground realities, Case Study has been undertaken to examine the reasons for no attendance in the Gram Sabhas and what exactly transpired in the Gram Sabhas.

Responses of Participants of Gram Sabha

A Scheduled Caste male who was in his mid-40s and a post-graduate without any job had admitted to having attended the village open meeting. He recalled that the issue discussed in this meeting (one year back) was 'singling', i.e., stone laying of the kutcha roads. He had also raised many questions in the Sabha pertaining to the unequal distribution of funds across the wards. He concluded by saying that the meeting was akin to a formal get-together of the elected members and their supporters as it was largely one-sided in terms of its composition (attendance) and activities (the agendas under discussed and issues taken up). When asked more specifically as to what exactly happened in the course of the meeting, he said, "the Pradhan delivered a long speech in which he made an inventory of the development and relief work the GP had undertaken during the past year. Besides, he also made a brief mention of the works undertaken under the Manipur Rural Employment Guarantee Scheme (MREGS). This went on almost two hours, during which the GP peon, holding the open Panchayat register in his hands, approached all those who were in the assembly and even passers-by and collected their signatures".

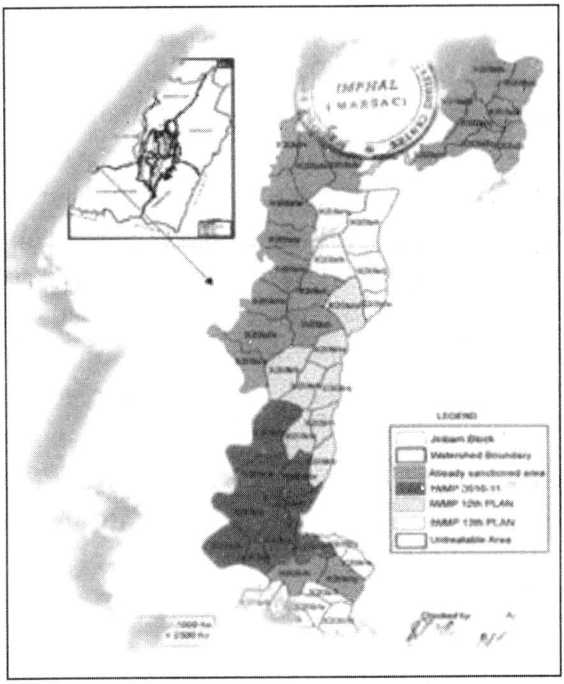

Map 3.3: Map of Tellou Channa Seijang Gram Panchayat

Gram Sabha Meeting in Open Ground

Another male in his mid-30s belonging to the Scheduled Tribe community, a graduate and unemployed (he was a formal Pradhan of Tellou Channa Seijang GP) was asked whether Gram Sabha meetings were held during his term. He said due to partisan politics and a 'strong lobby' system, he could not have obtained cooperation from the Panchayat members regarding this issue.[23] Nevertheless, he said, he attended the Gram Sabha meeting out of curiosity when genuine move was initiated in this regard for the first time. When asked about his observation on the Gram Sabha meeting, he said the Sabha was akin to a road show and nothing substantial was undertaken in it except the long speeches made by the Pradhan and some prominent Ward members.[24]

Responses of Non-Participants

People who normally do not go to Gram Sabha meetings offered several explanations. These included 'lack of time', 'not being informed', 'women do not go to open meeting', 'attended by spouses', and 'useless, trivial exercise and hence a waste of time'. Those who were educated (usually upper caste, prosperous farmers, or engaged in some business or white collar job) were almost contemptuous of the very notion of the village assembly. They kept themselves aloof from the affairs of the Gram Panchayat, including the Gram Sabha, which, they considered as an extended arm of a party-managed road show, not as people's forum.

In Tellou Channa Seijang, most people honestly admitted that they did not have the time for GS meeting. Women respondents who had never turned up for a meeting hopelessly countered with a question: "what women would do there"? The view that implies in this statement was that the Sabha is essentially a male domain where women's presence not to speak of their participation, was not appreciated. Then there were women, mostly poor and illiterate, who had expressed their lack of interest in the Sabha. They had seen the worthlessness of the Gram Sabha as an institution. To them there was no useful purpose in going to the Gram Sabha meeting when they had already known that nothing concrete would come out of it. Majority of the people had pleaded ignorance, implying their own fault, or complained that they were not informed.

That, political parties have used Panchayats as platforms to increase support base at the local level and that the party reaps electoral dividends in exchange for the favours it extends to its voters, is a common phenomenon in electoral politics. In that respect, what one notice in Tellou Channa Seijang Gram Panchayat is not uncommon. In Tellou Channa Seijang Gram Panchayat, national political party [CPI (M)] cadres spend great deal of their time in reaching out to the people and cultivating them, which in turn enables the consolidation of the social support base of the party.[25] There are many situations where the intervention of the Gram Panchayat becomes prerequisite. Yet not all can be obliged with such instruments of patronage. The problem gets compounded when public goods are not found in proper shape or where the collective interest gets affected. For instance, the main road in the Tellou Chenna Seijang Gram Panchayat was in bad shape, despite having been repaired twice earlier. The villagers were angry with its pathetic condition and many of them voiced their resentment against the way the repair work was done. The same is true of providing an electric connection in the hamlets not covered so far under the rural electrification programme. The Pradhan of Tellou Channa Seijang Gram Panchayat even confessed that it took a lot of time for her to get a new ration card. Thus, if anyone is to be blamed for the delay, it is the concerned department officials, not the Panchayat.[26] However, the people could not comprehend this point.

Accountability Mechanisms of Gram Panchayat

Gram Sabhas and accounts audits are not found in Tellou Channa Seijang Gram Panchayat. The Panchayat has not incorporated elements of citizens, audit or social audit either in the Gram Sabha.[27] Measures to enhance transparency and accountability were not instituted within the functioning of the Panchayati Raj institutions.[28]

The Manipur Panchayati Raj Act 2004 has provisions for the participation of citizens in planning and made it a requirement that the reasons in support of a decision should be evident, with sufficient information made available to the public. It has a provision for the increase in participation of the people in the decision-making process and minimizes the role of bureaucracy in the implementation of development programmes. However, in reality, there existed no institutional mechanism for the people/citizens to file petitions on any irregularities in the planning and implementation of the development programmes.

Added to this was the relatively low awareness among the people of the various measures of accountability. Regarding performance audits, they were intended to be independent of government control and to have their own standards. Despite this, the audits were conducted by State government officials, thereby reducing the scope for independent functioning. The performance audit is meant to be a corrective mechanism, and the Panchayat officials were of the view that it was more of a facilitating exercise. In its actual working, the report that is produced is not a public document, although elected representatives have access to it. Despite the emphasis on transparency, information on official performance continues to be a closed area.

Formation of beneficiary committees to implement public works was another important measure. According to the Manipur Panchayati Raj Act 2004, after the plan document is approved, Gram Sabhas/Ward committees should be convened to discuss the project to be implemented. A committee of 15 people and a chairperson is to be constituted by the Gram Sabhas. The beneficiary committees enter into agreement with the Gram Panchayats, and were paid the expenses of the project in instalments with a periodic review by the expert committee. Implementation through beneficiary committees is intended to minimize the role of contractors and intermediaries in carrying out public works, and enable speedy completion of the work that is undertaken. While the idea is well conceived, the extent to which it succeeds in containing corruption largely depends on the nature of the formation of these committees and their effectiveness.

In Tellou Channa Seijang Gram Panchayat, the beneficiary committees existed only on paper for the purpose of official records. The individuals listed as members did not take any interest in the actual implementation of public works. The formation of beneficiary committees was also not based on formal rules and procedures. They were formed without any consultation in the Gram Sabhas. Citizens were also not aware of the existence of beneficiary committees. Although the main aim of the beneficiary committees was to minimize the role of intermediaries, it was found that the public works, in most cases were awarded to the contractors. The representatives were of the opinion that it was not possible for the beneficiary committee members to take time off to fulfil the administrative procedures, and get clearance from the technical committee. The beneficiary committees in Tellou Channa Seijang Gram Panchayat was only a cover for the engineer, contractor, and official and elected member's nexus in the implementation of the development work.

Pertaining to beneficiary selection, the Panchayat has not developed any proper format. Beneficiary selection in Tellou Channa Seijang Gram Panchayat was done through formal announcements in loudspeaker.[29] In most cases where Gram Sabha meetings were conducted, either those who attended were reduced to being spectators or were consumers of the beneficiary programmes. Thus, Gram Sabhas failed to be a deliberative forum and channel of communication between the representatives and the constituents, and far from being an effective means of accountability. Except for the members of the Gram Panchayat and prospective beneficiaries in government programmes who attended the Gram Sabha meetings in their village, the people at large, did not attend the Gram Sabha meetings. Therefore, the citizens could not use Gram Sabhas as a forum to demand governance that is more effective.

Measures were neither institutionalized for greater transparency in decision-making in governance. All the Plan documents, papers related to prioritization of beneficiaries, bills and vouchers of public expenditure are not open to public scrutiny and/or reference. While it is also mandatory that the statement of expenses and other important details of public works be displayed at the site in Manipuri (the local language), it was not successful as a source of information as information was only displayed in English and that too, for a day to fulfil the requirements, and was removed later. At the same time, cases where members of the public objected to lapses in transparency have not been encountered in the course of the study.

Beneficiaries in Panchayat Pradhan's House Panchayat Office

District Planning Committee

Section 96 of the Manipur Panchayati Raj Act 1994 provides for the constitution of the District Planning Committee. Under this provision of the law, the government will constitute a District Planning Committee with the twin functions to consolidate the plans prepared by the Zilla Parishad, Gram Panchayats, Nagar Panchayats, Municipal Councils and Municipal Corporations; and to prepare a draft development plan for the district as a whole through this process of consolidation for the urban and the local areas (GoI 2006).

So far, District Planning Committees are constituted in two Districts out of four in Manipur and the Adhyaksha of Zilla Parishad is the chairperson of District Planning Committees. In those two districts that have such committees, a fifth of the total number of members are nominated, leading to the domination of civil servants and higher level politicians (such as the local MP and MLA). Being only partly elected, the committee is not accountable to the people, and can easily become a rival power centre. It is supposed to facilitate the use of expertise and technical skill of officials in the preparation of plans, but it becomes difficult in practice to combine or balance the principles of expertise with those of democracy and accountability.

Transparency in Local Governance

First, the mechanism which could ensure transparency at Gram Panchayat level are, Gram Sabha meetings, publication, local medias, news broadcast and various prominent places like notice board of Panchayat, village market, school compound, playground, etc.

Gram Panchayat in Tellou Channa Seijang has not followed any of these mechanisms due to political influence of the ruling party apparently for the fear that if it was done so, people would seek to know about many issues regarding budget, expenditure, beneficiary list, etc., for which offering proper response would be difficult on the part of the officials or representatives since the records and documents were not prepared properly.

Secondly, performance audits are intended to be independent of government control and to have their own standards. Despite this, the audits are conducted by State government officials, thereby reducing the scope for independent functioning. The performance audit is meant to be a corrective mechanism, and the Panchayat officials were of the view that it was more of a facilitating exercise. In its actual working, the report that is produced is not a public document, although elected representatives have access to it. Despite the emphasis on transparency, information on official performance continues to be a closed area.

Another important factor identified is the socio-cultural nature of the people. People themselves were not interested to know about the records, expenses or documents of Gram Panchayat. They emphasized more on individual relationship with the political leaders and were more interested in getting benefits from the Gram Panchayats through their political links. Once they benefited they were not interested to come to the Gram Panchayat office for second time. Panchayat functionaries were also fairly aware about issues like funding sources, standing committees, and State plan schemes but were unable to comprehend properly their own role as well as the role of the Gram Sabhas. The selection of beneficiaries had been carried out mostly outside the Gram Sabhas. Panchayats had failed to give due publicity of different poverty alleviation programmes to the people. Manipulation in the selection of target households and the schemes for public works was found to be common in all the sampled Panchayats. Corruption was rampant in the process for including households. The entire implementation process was found to be dominated by the contractors. This had prevented the local workforce from taking advantage of the wage employment opportunity.

Fourthly, the dominance over and capture of village Panchayats by the bureaucracy and the local elites had reduced the Panchayats to arenas of contestation for the spoils of office. The 'capture' phenomenon,[30] besides helping the elites to sustain class, caste, and gender discrimination, has also affected the performance of development programmes as it has evidently introduced a non-poor bias into the working of the Panchayats. One result of the 'capture' of the Panchayats is rank nepotism and a growing nexus between leaders and officials at different levels for sharing the spoils of office.

A 'culture of commission' seems to have pervaded development works. Misappropriation and leakage of funds is widespread, especially in places where a strong nexus between leaders, officials and contractors exists. In many cases, major portions of the programme funds are diverted for paying bribes and commissions, resulting in a highly unsatisfactory impact on the works. Capture of the Panchayats by local elites and the bureaucracy is compounded by the prevailing 'percentage culture' under which 6 to 7 per cent of development funds has been deducted as insurgency tax.

Fifthly, hasty implementation and manipulation of records have been commonly observed due to problems like untimely release of funds and mismatches between sanctioning cash and kind components. The continuation of many design flaws in many of the poverty alleviation programmes does not seem to have helped the Panchayats in reducing the distortions seen in the implementation. The problem has also been compounded because only limited importance is given to the involvement of Panchayats in the planning process. The involvement of Panchayats primarily in the implementation process has reduced their status to one of mere agents expected to meet the annual physical and financial targets given from above. Even if the Panchayats were to have any local developmental needs or compulsions, the agency role has greatly curtailed the scope for these local bodies to take any initiatives based on such requirements.

Finally, the presence of parallel bodies, promoted by both government and non-governmental organizations (NGOs) also seem to have diluted the significance of Gram Sabhas. Some safeguards involving the Gram Sabhas such as beneficiary committees and vigilance committees do not seem to have worked because of the weakening of Gram Sabha itself. This in turn has weakened the basic mechanism for ensuring transparency and accountability in the functioning of Panchayats.

Integrated Analyses

The Panchayat studied plays its role as implementing agency and elected representatives do not build skill for formation of plan and do not feel confidence over their duty. Besides this, people lose faith in elected bodies and become closer to party leaders.

The Gram Panchayat covers a population of about 3,000 spread over 15 villages. Obviously such small units may not lend themselves to holistic planning and cannot afford to have significant technical support to plan or implement a scheme. No plan worthy of the name can be prepared at this level and what is submitted by them to the higher level panchayats can only be a set of demands.

Regarding people's participation, the overall picture that has emerged is somewhat akin to the unfinished task of decentralization, irrespective of the lifespan of decentralized Panchayati Raj institutions in the State. People took active participation in Panchayat elections thinking that their votes matter a lot to decide the fate of a government, which through their active intervention in the form of election would effectively deliver services to them. Yet, they are not aware of the functioning of this very government. The explanation to this phenomenon could be that the presence of Panchayati Raj institutions is widely recognized by the people; they are educating the people and are playing a role in the development of rural infrastructure, but not serving all intended functions, as demonstrated by their inability to foster transparency, accountability and participation.

Secondly, participation in Gram Sabha meetings is largely low in the study of Panchayat. The point that the Gram Sabha is entrusted with a larger functional domain is blurred with its mistaken identity as a forum for the disbursement of state largesse.

Most of the Gram Panchayat members do not have understanding of the powers and responsibilities given to them under the Act. Sometimes, Pradhans do not involve Up-Pradhans and members of the opposition in decision-making process. In order to avoid their involvement in decision-making about selection of proposals, Pradhans usually try to get the proposals approved in the general meetings, which are mostly dominated people close to the Pradhan and those who expect to be selected as beneficiaries of the various Central and State sponsored schemes.

The Manipur Panchayati Raj Act 2004 has provisions for the participation of citizens in planning and made it a requirement that the reasons in support of a decision should be evident, with sufficient information made available to the public. It has a provision for the increase in participation of the people in the decision-making process and minimizes the role of bureaucracy in the implementation of development programmes. However, in reality, there existed no institutional mechanism for the people/citizens to file petitions on any irregularities in the planning and implementation of the development programmes.

Added to this was the relatively low awareness of among the people of the various measures of accountability. Regarding performance audits, they were intended to be independent of government control and to have their own standards. Despite this, the audits were conducted by State government officials, thereby reducing the scope for independent functioning. The performance audit is meant to be a corrective mechanism, and the Panchayat officials were of the view that it was more of a facilitating exercise. In its actual working, the report that is produced is not a public document, although elected representatives have access to it. Despite the emphasis on transparency, information on official performance continues to be a closed area.

A number of efforts have been undertaken to impart training to Panchayat leaders. However, efforts undertaken have only a limited impact and fall definitely short of their possible potential. The overall perspective remains largely patriarchal and patronizing. The underlying assumption being that most people who have entered the local government, particularly the women, OBCs and other marginalized communities (SCs/STs) have come in with no skills and no knowledge. The training efforts — both in content as well as process, thus, treats the elected representatives of local government as ignorant and passive recipients of new knowledge. Secondly, most of the trainings have targeted the Pradhans, Zilla Parishad members and the Gram Sevaks. Gram Sabha members, Ward members and local government officials are mostly left out of these initiatives. Third, capacity building has been, by and large, delivered through structured indoor trainings. Except for a very few exceptions, most of the content has been targeted towards a literate trainee, whereas, a large majority of local representatives are in fact functionally non-literate. Moreover, challenged by the large-scale numbers to be covered, the training efforts have mostly continued to be one time in the entire duration and limited in reach and scope in terms of the content and pedagogy. Fourthly, there is little systematic networking and collaboration between efforts made by the government and civil society organizations. Thus, there is a lot of duplication of effort, and also a sub-optimal use of resources.

Conclusion

To conclude, Tellou Channa Gram Panchayat has generally failed as an institution of local self government principally because of the following reasons:

First, the necessary devolution of functionaries, functions, and funds has not taken place. Secondly, people's participation in decentralized governance is largely low. Third, the Gram Sabha in its present set-up has a limited role to play (*The point that the Gram Sabha is entrusted with a larger functional domain is blurred with its mistaken identity as a forum for the disbursement of state largesse*). Fourth, the mechanisms of accountability, transparency are not up to the desirable level. Fifth, the creation/continuance of parallel bodies for planning and implementation of development schemes at the local level has hurt the functioning of the PRIs (*There is a serious problem of overlap/substitution at both Zilla Parishad as well as Gram Panchayat levels*). Finally, capacity building of the Panchayat leaders is extremely low.

Unwillingness of the State Government to give out power to the panchayats remains the most important factor responsible for such a dismal state of the panchayats. Gram Panchayats were virtually made as an agent of senior leaders of the ruling party.

Aiding to the excessive centralization and bureaucratization was the issue of elite capture of the Panchayat. The dominance over and capture of village Panchayats by the bureaucracy and the local elites had reduced the Panchayats to arenas of contestation for the spoils of office.

The creation and continuance of parallel bodies for planning and implementation of development schemes at the local level has hurt the functioning of the Panchayati Raj Institutions (PRIs). Indeed, the establishment of such parallel bodies in the early years of the newly established local bodies of self-governance has stunted the development of these institutions in several instances. Often these parallel bodies represented processes external to the constitutionally mandated role of the PRIs and enabled the bureaucracy and MPs/MLAs to override the authority of democratically elected members of PRIs.

Most importantly, the more than two decades long state of militant violence in the State has not only gravely affected the normal functioning of governments at the local level but also provided an alibi for public officials not to perform. Manipur with a population of 30,23,141 (2001 Census) is perhaps, the State with the highest per capita "terrorist organization" not only in India but the whole world. Of the 28 militant organizations branded as "Terrorist" in India under POTA, ten are from the North-East region out of which again six are from Manipur. Fratricidal fighting among these different insurgent groups has not only gravely affected the normal functioning of governance both at the State and local levels but also seriously eroded the civil society space. In fact, militant violence has contributed largely towards the shrinking of the democratic space and in silencing the voice of the civil society. There is no scope for any democratic space in the very organizational structure and mode of functioning of the insurgent groups and the average citizen has nowhere to appeal in case of insurgent violence. The unresolved question of insurgency and economic stagnancy moves in a vicious circle. The economic stagnancy that impedes employment and income growth serves as fertile ground for fortifying and sustaining insurgency. On the other hand, the growing militancy and the subsequent growth of the underground terrorist economy, backed by the disruptive power of the militants, distort and inhibit the processes of growth of legitimate economic and developmental activities. The civil society along with a wide variety of economic activities that were integral to the lives of the people of Manipur have been 'criminalized', forcing otherwise law abiding citizens into a collusive relationship with militants within their areas of influence. Moreover, militant groups gradually usurp a wide range of governmental functions, including the (albeit conditional) perfection of life and property, and the provision of 'justice' to local communities.

Added to the phenomenon of insurgency and economic stagnancy, numerous civil-society protests in the form of bands and strikes, partial or total at the slightest provocation, have become frequent phenomenon. Throw into these mixes the question of governability and we have the enduring challenge that the State of Manipur face today.

To complicate matters is the half-hearted and unsystematic arrangement of the system of self-governance in the State. Although small population is in question, two systems of local government are in operation in Manipur and that too sometimes in contravention of the broad theoretical premise that dictated the criteria (Partha S. Ghosh, 2008). The two systems are: Autonomous District Council under the Manipur Hill Areas, District Councils Act 1975, but not under the Sixth Schedule of the Constitution of India, and the Panchayati Raj Institutions as per the 73rd Amendment of the Indian Constitution.

Policy Recommendations

Gram Panchayats should be empowered to collect local toll and taxes by facilitating more public utilities. Lack of role clarity and lack of support staff are important factors explaining low level of revenue for the Panchayats. Hence, effective devolution of functions and functionaries is requirement for effective devolution of finances. Parallel channels of flow of funds like MP Funds and MLA funds should not be merged with Panchayat funds.

Gram Sabha (GS) should be strengthened. Powers and functions of the Gram Sabha should be spelt out in great detail, articulating its role as planner, decision-maker and auditor. A massive awareness creation programme should be organized to inform Gram Sabha about its role in planning, implementation, audit of development programmes, and in control of natural resources, land records and conflict resolution. Modalities should be evolved where those who want to participate in PRIs are facilitated. The practice in some States of providing for people's assemblies below the Gram Sabha needs to be widely adopted. Party-based Panchayat election should be discouraged. Regarding accountability, Gram Panchayats should be encouraged and empowered to collect local toll and taxes by facilitating more public utilities. Local taxation is the best check that people can exercise over their own elected Panchayat representatives. The cycle of accountability is complete when people know what they want, what Panchayats have, what they should have and what they should pay so that Panchayats can deliver what they want. The right to recall should be brought into existence. Voter need not wait for five years to replace a leader who is not an effective representative.

Regular Gram Sabha is essential to ensure that all records and documents including audit report, income and expenditure account of the Gram Panchayat are placed in the meeting for discussion and published as annual report of the Gram Panchayat for distribution to the people. There is also an urgent need for working to strengthen Social Audits. To conduct Social Audit in its true form, the community needs to make demand for it.

Capacity building initiatives must be undertaken with full respect for skills and strengths that Panchayat functionaries bring with them. The impact of capacity building processes should be evaluated to ensure that these are targeted to the real and felt needs of the functionaries. It will help ensure that the process, content and methodology of capacity building efforts are suited and relevant to the context. It is important to build a database of who has been trained and for what: such data could be made universally available through IT network. Such a data will also strengthen accountability and ensure capacity building funds are spent for the purpose in an optimal manner. There may be a need to institutionalize collaborations with other agencies, such as SHGs, NGOs, CBOs, and Youth Clubs, etc.

REFERANCES

1. *See* The Manipur Panchayati Raj Act 1994, Ss. 3(1) and 15 r/w S. 2 (h) and (S).
2. *See* The Manipur Panchayati Raj Act 1994, S. 4.
3. *See* The Manipur Panchayati Raj Act 1994, S. 5.
4. *See* The Manipur Panchayati Raj Act 1994, S. 9.
5. *See* The Manipur Panchayati Raj Act 1994, S.12.

6. *See* The Manipur Panchayati Raj Act 1994, S.13-14, S.19-20, Ss.15-18, 21 and 26.
7. *See Ibid.* S. 35.
8. *See* The Manipur Panchayati Raj Act 1994, S. 36.
9. *Ibid.* S. 40.
10. *Ibid.* S. 49.
11. *Ibid.* S. 52.
12. *Ibid.* S. 53.
13. *Ibid.* S. 61.
14. The Manipur Panchayati Raj Act 1994, S. 61.
15. *Ibid.*, S. 62.
16. *Ibid.*, S. 63.
17. *Ibid.*, S. 71.
18. *Ibid.* S. 72.
19. The Manipur Panchayati Raj Act, S. 73 and 74.
20. The Manipur Panchayati Raj Act, 1994 S. 70
21. *Ibid.* S. 80.
22. *Ibid.*, S. 96.
23. There exists a community-wise division within and amongst the elected representatives. Being an ST, he was sidelined on many issues as majority of the Ward members belong to the majority community.
24. Ward members who were close to the Pradhan have a more important role in the proceedings of the Gram Sabha meeting and were seen to be 'more prominent'.
25. Even though elected representatives at the local level are usually not elected on party lines, party affiliations of elected members in this Panchayat were very strong. Ward members were equally divided into two camps in terms of their Party affiliation. The Pradhan along with five Ward members were strong supporters of the CPI(M) whereas, the remaining 7 Ward members were strong supporters of INC. In most cases, decisions were made by the Pradhan along with those Ward members who were her supporters.

26. The State government was not willing to devolve functions to the Panchayats. As per the record of Activity mapping approved by the cabinet, 16 functions have been devolved to the local body institutions, but in reality, only 6 functions were devolved to the Panchayats. The State government departments have taken up almost all the functions with the Panchayats having been reduced to the level of being only the implementing agency of the State government departments.
27. In a personal interview with Ward member of Tellou Channa Seijang Gram Panchayat, who was also a Deputy Pradhan of the same Panchayat, it was revealed that Gram Sabha meetings have never been conducted in 10 (ten) years.
28. There is no Panchayat office, not to talk of notice boards. Gram Panchayat meetings were usually held in the Pradhan's house.
29. Loudspeakers were provided to Ward members as material component under NREGS. Using these loudspeakers, Ward members made formal announcements (in their respective Wards), of the distribution of applications for Job Cards. Interestingly enough, it was found, in the course of field study, that one particular household in Laipham Khunnou Gram Parishad has five members holding job cards while another household (with seven members) has no single member holding job card. There were a number of complaints about the beneficiary selection, indicating greater public awareness of NREGS, and protests against the politics of patronage.
30. Included in this phenomenon is also the 'percentage culture', where fixed percentage of all the development funds sanctioned to the different levels of the Panchayats has been deducted as 'Insurgency Tax'.

NOTES

Anand. 2008. "The State of Panchayats: 2007-08: An Independent Assessment". Vol. I & II, *Institute of Rural Management (IRMA),* MoPR, GoI, New Delhi.

Aziz, Abdul and David, D. Arnold (eds.). 1996. "*Decentralised Governance in Asian Countries*". New Delhi: Sage Publications.

Chaturvedi, T.N. 1998. "Accountability: The Concept and its Significance". In Raj, K. Nigam (ed.), *Public Accountability in Indian Polity*. New Delhi:D.C. Publication.

Cheema, G.S., and D. A. Rondinelli. (eds.). 1983. "*Decentralisation and Development: Policy Implementation in Developing Countries*". Beverly Hills: Sage Publications.

Crook Richard and James Manor. 1998. *Democracy and Decentralization in South Asia and West Africa: Participation, Accountability and Performance*. London: Cambridge University Press.

Ghosh K. 2001. "Transparency in Panchayats: West Bengal Scenario." *Administrative Change*, XXVIII (2): 69-80.

GoM (Government of Manipur). 1960. *The United Provinces Panchayats Act 1947*. Manipur Gazette No. 177-E-130: Imphal.

GoM (Government of Manipur). 1975. *The Manipur Panchayati Raj Act 1976*. Directorate of Rural Development and Panchayati Raj: Imphal.

GoM (Government of Manipur). 1994. *The Manipur Panchayati Raj Act 1994*. Directorate of Rural Development and Panchayati Raj: Imphal.

GoM (Government of Manipur). 1996. *Report of the Manipur State Finance Commission*. Imphal.

GoM (Government of Manipur). 2000. *Government Order No. 9/13/95 – Development – (P)/pt – III (A). dt. 13 June* (on Devolution of Functions to PRIs).

GoM (Government of Manipur). 2006. *Status Note of PRIs in Manipur*. Planning Department: Imphal.

GoM (Government of Manipur). 2008. *Economic Survey of Manipur (2008-09)*. Directorate of Economics and Statistics. Imphal.

GoM (Government of Manipur). 2008. *Manipur State Budget 2009-09*. Finance Department: Imphal.

GoM (Government of Manipur). 2008. *Statistical Abstracts of Manipur 2002*. Directorate of Economic and Statistics: Imphal.

GoM (Government of Manipur). 2009. *Annual Administrative Report (2008-09)*. Department of Rural Development & Panchayati Raj: Imphal.

Hargopal, G., and Sudarshanam, G. 2004. *Status of Panchayati Raj in the States and UTs of India*. ISS: Andhra Pradesh.

Kothari, Rajni. 1999. "Issues in Decentralised Governance." In S.N. Jha and P.C. Mathur (eds.), *Decentralization and Local Politics*. New Delhi: Sage Publications.

Maisam, N. 2008. "Decentralization for Development: The Panchayati Raj System in Two Districts of Manipur." *Thesis submitted to Calcutta University for the award of PhD*: Calcutta University.

Ministry of Panchayati Raj, Government of India. 2006. "Status of Panchayati Raj: State Profile Manipur." *The State of the Panchayats: A Mid-term Review and Appraisal*. November 22, Vol. II.

Palanithurai, G. 1997. "Capacity Building Exercise for Elected Representatives in Tamil Nadu." *Journal of Rural Development*, Vol. 16 (4), Hyderabad: National Institute of Rural Development.

Singh, M. Iboton. 2005. "Political Economy of Manipur: Transformation within the Mixed Economy Paradigm. *Eastern Quarterly*, Vol. No. 3 (3), pp. 170-182. Manipur Research Forum: New Delhi.

Sitakantha Sethi. 2006. "People's Participation in Decentralised Planning". In *Empowerment of Panchayati Raj Institutions in India*, New Delhi: Sarup & Sons.

Sujit, K. Dutta. 2004. "Perception of the Elected Representatives of PRIs on Poverty Alleviation Programmes: Some Lessons from Manipur". In *Decentralised Governance in India: Myth and Reality*, New Delhi: Deep & Deep Publications Pvt. Ltd.

Chapter IV

Analysis

While comparing local governance system of Germany with India, it is necessary to find commonalities and in the backdrop of the framework analysis has to be made. It is a known fact that local governance in Germany is in an industrial and urban setting and local governance in India is in a developing economy with rural setting. The basic objectives of local governance in India are totally different from that of Germany. Social settings are differing with each other. Yet there are commonalities. Local governance in Germany and India is in the hands of provincial government. In both countries institutional structures are in place permanently as Central and State Governments. Roles and responsibilities have been assigned to the local governance institutions. To perform the assigned responsibilities resource base has been created and through which resources have been mobilized. Our concern here is to look at the institutional structure from the perspective of its capability and service delivery.

While visualizing the Indian local governance, social setting should be kept in the backdrop. It is necessary that to what extent social transformation is being achieved by the efforts of the local governance as it is mandated in the

Constitution itself. Local bodies in the rural areas in India has to work for democratization of society. In the process of democratization of society, one will find more of conflict rather than harmony. High social conflict will affect democratic functioning of the institutions and delivery of services.

Second aspect is the delivery of services. Effective delivery of services depends on the professionalization of the institutional structures and the claim of the stakeholders. Extreme professionalism is needed only at the ground as institutions are delivering services to the people. Equally the stakeholders should have needed empowerment to claim their entitlements as rights. Though institutions are functioning in the two countries, character, nature, strength and capacity vastly differ from each other.

Local governance practices have their own history in both countries. There had been many organizational and institutional arrangements along with local governments in both countries. Local governance in Germany and India are regulated as per the framework evolved by the provincial governments. In terms of autonomy and independence the local bodies of Germany have been enjoying the full autonomy without the influence of the state and federal governments. Whereas in India even though it has been created through a constitutional provision, local bodies could not enjoy such autonomy as enjoyed by the German local bodies. In terms of the workload the German local bodies are having defined workload people in Germany are least government. Many of the responsibilities are with the people themselves. Local bodies in Germany are facilitating the people to engage themselves and making them to enjoy life. In India, Local bodies have to provide basic services to the people. People are struggling to get adequate essential services from the local bodies.

Administrative reform process for local governance is going on in both countries. The difference between the German government and Indian government is the seriousness with which activities are carried out. In India we have documents prepared by the experts to reform local governance. Yet steps have not been taken either at the federal government level or at the State government level. In normal practice viability of a local institution is looked at from management perspective for effective delivery of services and management of the institution. Germany demonstrated the fact that even a small village can manage on its own as long as its financial viability is ensured. Whereas in India small village Panchayat survives on the grant given by the State and Central governments. Resource base of the German local bodies is sound. Since many of the services are paid, collecting resources from the people is not a problem in Germany. People have developed a healthy practice that services are to be paid. No service is free in Germany. Even poor will pay for every service. Local bodies need not bother to look after many services as they are paid and they are being delivered by different agencies. In India all basic services are to be provided by the local bodies and they are to be provided free of cost. While delivering services, services in Germany are extremely professional in nature as they got extreme professionalism on the part of the staff and agency working in the service organizations. In India it is very difficult to see such professionalism at the ground. Sanitation was intact in the culture of the society in Germany, maintaining cleanliness is not a problem. Whereas in India we have toilets but there is no sanitation culture and as a result we face problems. In Germany local body has to concentrate much on maintaining library, community halls, and other facilities for community gathering and conducting various kinds of activities.

The major workload of local bodies lies in providing basic services to the people in India whereas in Germany the local bodies have to facilitate people to enjoy life. Basic facilities are assured as they are paid with quality. People not only lead decent human life, but also dignified and enjoyable life. In India, though the local bodies are providing basic facilities, people are not able to lead a decent dignified human life as there is no such culture and practice. People have to devote enough time to get their entitlements even though they are assured of free of cost. Thus life becomes difficult and struggleful. But in Germany life is decent, dignified and enjoyable. Adherence to rules, regulations and laws is common. One can see the rule and act accordingly. It is only rule of law and not the rule of ruling party or rule of the leader in Germany. In India local bodies are leader centric and ruling party centric. Rule of law does not have a role.

Literacy is cent per cent in Germany. Health status is excellent. Hence, on these areas the local body need not concentrate in Germany. Further there is no intense social conflict. Equality and equity are well managed. They are part of the political culture. In India on all the areas the local body has to work. Since local bodies are enjoying autonomy, they take innovative initiatives in Germany. In the case study of village Holzheims, the local body has forged partnership with communities around the world. They sign MoU with local bodies of other countries. This case study local body has signed MoU with the local body Giciye in sector Birembura of Rwanda. They visit Rwanda and exchange ideas and help Rwanda. Primarily and crucially capacity of the system, capacity of the elected representatives and the level of awareness among the people about governance and development are important for the development of the communities in the villages.

In Germany the community as well as the elected representatives of the people in the local bodies are conscious of environmental issues. They discuss and regulate the same. Though they give permission to industries, they regulate the industries in terms of Green management and Waste management. They care for environmental protection and beauty of the village. Because all the social and cultural activities are performed only in the park and community hall areas.

In Indian context as per the record, local bodies have got enormous powers. But while checking the reality at the ground there is no correlation between the provisions in the Local Body Act and the actions of the Local Bodies. The capacity of the elected representatives is very low. Equally awareness level of the people about the local body system is poor. Enormous responsibilities have been given to the local bodies but to cope up with the responsibilities resources have not been given. To carry out the assigned roles and responsibilities the local body leaders should have capacity more than the capacity of the District Collector. Law of the subsidiarity works very well in Germany and not in India. Crucially the poor awareness level of the people about the local body system and the poor capacity of the elected representatives limiting the power of the local bodies. If the above two factors are taken care of, local bodies in India will be strengthened.

Chapter V

Conclusion

With a general framework, consists of structure, powers, roles, responsibilities, resources and performance, two case studies have been undertaken in local governance in Germany and India. Both case studies have been undertaken in the lowest unit of local governance framework of both countries. While making an analysis broader background settings of the local governance arrangements in both countries have been given. Functioning of the local bodies of both countries from the case studies have been analyzed in the backdrop of the commonalities. It is noted that the local body system in Germany is in a different socio-economic setting compared to local body system in India. Assigned responsibility of democratization of society to the Indian local body system is the difficult job and for which the elected representatives should have needed capacity which is far greater than the capacity of the elected representatives of the local body system in Germany. Elected representative of the local bodies in India should have more capacity than the capacity of their counter parts in Germany as they have to discharge dual responsibilities of democratization and development of communities. Democratizing the higher archical society is stupendous task. Equally achieving development by providing basic services is also very difficult. In Germany it is only managerial and supervisory.

Further, while looking at the responsibilities assigned to local bodies in India as per the Constitution one would wonder whether the whole system of governance in India is evolved from the bottom. In such a way constitutionally local bodies are created. But to carry out the assigned duties and responsibilities follow up activities at the federal and provincial government levels are very limited. As Constitution gives promises to the poor for the sixty years, the local bodies in India are giving only promises but they are not fulfilled. But there are enough potential in local bodies. To use the potentials, the stakeholders should have needed awareness and empowerment. In reality it is not so. Awareness of the public about the potentials of the system and the capacity of the elected representatives are also limited and poor in Indian context.

Moreover, the officials working at the grassroots are not professionally equipped to deliver the services effectively and efficiently. Resources to local bodies are also limiting factors. Contrary to India, Germany exhibits a sound local body system with adequate responsibilities with role clarity. Follow up actions are to the level of expectations. Functionaries working in the local government are highly professionals. Resource mobilization capacity of the local bodies is more and services are paid. Hence, local bodies are with local bodies of other countries. It is demonstrated that local governance is for local populace to lead a decent and dignified human life. In India, decentralization is very sound in documents but poor in practice.

Index